THE RIDE OF A LIFETIME

The Making of Mighty Ruthie

Ruthie Bolton

Copyright ©2012
Pathworks Publishing
Sacramento, California

Photographs from the Ruthie Bolton Collection

The experiences recounted in this book are true.

Publisher's Cataloging-in-Publication Data

Bolton, Ruthie, 1967-

The ride of a lifetime : the making of mighty Ruthie / by Ruthie Bolton.

p. cm.

ISBN: 978-0-9777280-0-8

1. Women basketball players —United States—Biography. 2. Women's National Basketball Association. 3. African American basketball players—Biography. 4. Ability in children. 5. Education—Parent participation. I. Title.

GV884.B656 A3 2012

796.323`092—dc22

2011945512

The paper used in this publication meets minimum requirements of the American National Standard for Information Sciences—Permanence of Paper for Printed Library Materials: ANSI Z39.48-1992.

Printed in Minneapolis, Minnesota

Set in Adobe Caslon Pro

Designed by Anthony Sclavi

Printed in the United States of America.

10 9 8 7 6 5 4 3 2 1

THE RIDE OF A LIFETIME

CONTENTS

PREFACE

One of the most powerful things we can do is share our stories. As time passes on, we recognize how positive, uplifting stories motivate and help others along their unique and extraordinary paths. Everyone has an extraordinary story to develop, experience and share.

This is my story—a ride that started when I entered the world in McLain, Mississippi. I had no idea my "ride" would yield such fantastic experiences. I believe it did because I opened myself to the possibilities and ignored the naysayers and those who had little faith along the way. I had faith in myself and in my Maker. My dad, a Baptist preacher, always told me, "Daughter, life is 10% what happens to you and 90% how you respond to it." I never doubted this truth. I believed it with my entire being. It picked me up when I was down. I practiced the art of never giving up and believing deeply. I hold my father in the highest esteem for instilling this wonderful work ethic and enduring, hopeful spirit in me. His light sparked mine.

I believe that hard work and dedication leads to the fulfillment of our dreams, no matter what anyone may tell you. This is a proactive truth—not a cliché. I lived and practiced this principle on my journey and it took me places I never dreamed of, nor ever thought of as a possibility for me or any of my nineteen brothers and sisters. The day I stood in the White House and shook the hand of the President of the United States of America, I was filled with overwhelming emotion and a knowing that one of my dreams was fulfilled. When I returned to the White House again after our second Olympic Gold medal basketball championship, I knew that my perseverance, endurance and focus led to success rather than a dream deferred. I was living, not worrying about my dream. I had nurtured my talents and it led to positive rewards. We must invest in our dreams and sometimes that is not easy or comfortable.

True, life happens. But you must always remember that you are the director in charge of your life outcomes. My dad always reminded us that with God all things are possible. He would always say, "If you take with you in life just a few principles, you don't have to carry a suitcase full of rules." But, I learned that without faith, perseverance, dedication, commitment, self-discipline and hard work, some possibilities remain tucked away like an unopened present in your closet.

This book combines elements of my life story with the positive advice I give youngsters in an effort to motivate them to work hard and achieve the best for themselves. The book is designed to help young people develop a solid foundation, including confidence, a strong work ethic, and positive self-esteem. Some children may not come from loving, two-parent homes. They may hang out with the wrong crowds on the street. This book is designed to help them make more positive choices and achieve their own dreams instead of falling prey to negative peer pressures. I tell my story to let them see the things I had to overcome on my journey, emphasizing the great foundation I received from my dad and how his advice enabled me to never give up, to persevere even when things looked bleak.

We all have many gifts. Discover them. Open them. Refine them. Nurture them. They will lead to a life more fully experienced—a ride of a lifetime better than you ever imagined. This is why I share my story. Enjoy it and "open up" to your own possibilities.

Peace and blessings,

Ruthie Bolton

ACKNOWLEDGEMENTS

First, I would like to thank the Lord for using basketball as a platform for me to share my journey with young people and for choosing me as your vessel. In the bible Luke (12:48) says: "To whom much is given much is required." To give back to the community in this way is a special gift I treasure. I also wish to acknowledge and thank several individuals who have contributed to the preparation of this book. First, Bill Gutman, my co-writer who spent countless hours helping me share my journey with others. I could not have done it without you. Thanks, Bill. Also, I wish to thank the many photographers who snapped photos of the highlights of my career, particularly Felicia Rule and Robert Maryland. Special thanks to Up N In Sports, LLC particularly the kindness and generosity of Brian Blackwell, who invested in my vision. You have truly been an amazing friend and I look forward to our continued work together.

To the staff at Pathworks Business Development, Inc., and particularly to Dr. Melissa Brown, I wish to say thanks for your devoted commitment and the countless hours you spent helping me edit and finish this important milestone in my life. I have no words to express my gratitude; you were for sure Heaven sent! This is only our beginning. Special thanks to Blia Xiong, Madelyne Oliver and Anna Otis for their contributions. To Coach Joe Ciampi—thanks for making me dig deep to find the gold within. Special thanks to Coach Carol Ross from Mississippi, who recruited my sister Maeola to Auburn University and continued to support us throughout the years. Your friendship has meant so much. A great friend, supporter, and basketball advocate, Debbie McCloud, is owed a debt of gratitude for her long term commitment to the Ruthie Bolton Foundation.

I am thankful for being part of the Nike family. Nike believed in women's basketball, supported our Olympic Teams, and invested in the careers of so many women basketball players from the start. To Coach Tara Vanderveer and Coach Nell Fortner—thanks for helping us bring home the gold twice! Thanks for helping me fulfill my dream. Most importantly, thank you both for helping me with my six pack!

To the WNBA and Renee Brown—thanks for making my dreams and the dreams of so many talented female ball players come true. To the Maloofs—thank you so much for giving me and many other young women the opportunity to not only play the game, but also to give back to the community. My Monarchs experiences are unforgettable. To my friend, Nikki McCray thanks for believing in me and investing in my endeavor. Once again, you have been a great teammate. To all my former teammates and opponents, thanks for challenging me to rise to the next level. To Dave Ancrum, thanks for getting me in the lab and continuously refining my shot. Thanks to the Positive Coaches Alliance (PCA) for their double Gold work ethic that makes a sportsmanship difference for all of us.

To Steve and the Del Oro Eagles (Angels) basketball team, thanks for allowing me to be a part of the Del Oro family. Keep investing in the lives of those young ladies! I look forward to watching all of you thrive. To the William Jessup University, thanks for my first coaching debut. To Joan Carrington and Barbara I and Barbara II, our friendship was great and your cooking even better! To Petrie Byrd, my standup comedian, thanks for fueling my joy. Special thanks to the GEAR UP Program and Shelley Davis for giving me the opportunity to share my message with young people through your program. To my most resourceful friend, Tawanna Wright, thanks for answering my calls and helping me to be so organized! To Omar and Debra Turner and Crossover Basketball, thanks all your community involvement and encouragement of young people.

I am so thankful for the contributions of Lori Bluett, my new amazing friend. Also thanks for supporting and investing in my new endeavor to "make a difference." To my longtime friends, Angela Archie and Andrea Lepore, thanks for your friendship and management support. Ricardo Adams, your willingness to support my camps and coach young people made a big difference. To my D. J., Aman, keep making us move. Lee Govan, you are in a league of your own; together we will "Keep It Real." To the Roberts Family Development Center, your commitment to youth is terrific. Thanks for allowing me to help you transform lives. To Fran Barker, you have been like a mother to me. Thanks for all your words of wisdom.

Thanks to my prayer team for keeping me richly blessed: Karen Sweeting, Susan and Daniel Baker, Bishop and Charlene Carthen, Scott and Karen Hagen, Bob Balian, and John and Lilly Swan (my true prayer warrior). To Rose Perez and family, thanks for being there for me, cooking great meals and helping with the kids. To the "young" Dr. Bobby Jones, thanks for blessing America with great gospel music for the past 30 years. To Cinda Fox, thanks for being an amazing friend and supporting me through all the ups and downs. I love you so much. To the Elmasian family, thanks for your prayers and continuous love and support. To Ms.

Kay and Renee, thanks for your love and support and always having something for me to eat in the refrigerator!

To my Italian family, Franco, Beatrice, Magi, and Carlotta, grazie for sharing my amazing journey. I love you so much. I also want to thank my family, particularly my parents, the late Linwood and Leola Bolton who gave me such wonderful principles to live by that I share them with others throughout this book. I dedicate this book to them. My 19 brothers and sisters all helped me become the person I am today in their own unique way and for that I am grateful. Here they are: Earl, Katherine, Ceola, Linder Ruth, Betty Ann, Rose Marie, Linwood Jr., Lucille, James, Jessica, Byrone, Mary, Jerry, Paul, Maeola, Allen Ray, Nathaniel, Tanglyn, and Inez. Also thanks to my 115 nieces and nephews and my immediate family and in-laws who continue to fuel my passion. Special thanks to the Al and Dora Willis Family who became our family guardians and avid basketball fans. Your hospitality and love makes you champion Mississippians. Thanks to the Greenwood Family for helping me in so, so many ways. Special, special thanks to my fans—the people who nicknamed me "Mighty Ruthie"—for that and for the fond memories you gave me I will be eternally grateful. Above all, thanks to my loving family, Ceasar, Hope, and Christofer. I appreciate your patience and steadfast support and look forward to our continuing journey together.

Peace and blessings,

Ruthie Bolton

FOREWORD

It was the summer of 1985. I sat comfortably in my study reviewing my recruitment roster. A good line up of our recruits were being flown in and toured around our stately southern university. Ruthie Bolton wasn't on the list. In fact, she wasn't really on my radar screen.

Though I had recruited her sister Maeola Bolton the previous year, my associates and I had determined that younger sister Ruthie wasn't ready for big time college level play. When recruiting Maeola to play at Auburn University, I was intrigued by her sister, Ruthie's involvement in the game. She was the player who made her teammates better. She was the player making the passes to her teammates to score.

However, Maeola had proven herself on the team. She was quick and very athletic with amazing scoring ability. Maeola was the Bolton we needed. As a result of our relationship with Maeola, we became acquainted with the large Bolton family and their father, the Reverend Linwood Bolton. He was a terrific advocate for his family and was excited about the idea of possibly Maeola and Ruthie playing together. I felt Ruthie could play in my system but was concerned that she would be negatively affected by her limited playing time compared to Maeola's. However after she called about coming to Auburn University, sounding so excited, we decided to send for her on a bus and allowed her to come for a visit.

When Ruthie arrived, my wife and I invited her, Maeola and a few other players for dinner. After dinner, I felt compelled to tell Ruthie that this may not be the place for her. I told her that her playing time at Auburn University would have to be earned not awarded, and that she probably wouldn't even play until her junior year. She was dejected and speechless but I believed this frank notice was for the best. I told her we could help her get into another college. Ruthie went home the next day.

Surprisingly, we got a call a week later from Ruthie saying she was ready for the challenge. When pre-season began, we were surprised to see Ruthie's level of intensity and improvement as she fought for a spot on the team. She had become a contender like a butterfly emerging from a cocoon. My team coaches saw her resilience too. Her competitive drive showed me she was a special player.

When we posted the team roster that year, there were two Bolton's on the list—a totally unexpected, unplanned occurrence. Ruthie was a fighter and she made us see how hard work pays off. Ruthie had become an effective, smart player both on and off the court. She beat the odds and made the team in the fall of her freshman year! Ruthie became a leader on our team because of her work ethic, discipline, and love of her teammates.

The Bolton's helped us win three conference championships and make two final four appearances. It's amazing that it all started because the "Mighty Ruthie" as she later became known in the WNBA would not be denied. She taught us all a valuable lesson and went on to help the United States win two Olympic gold basketball championships.

Ruthie's alma matter, Auburn University and I take great pride in her achievements and encourage everyone to pursue their dreams despite the odds like Ruthie did. That's why we felt her jersey deserved to be retired at Auburn University a few years ago. Our Mighty Ruthie went on to WNBA greatness and made the big shots that created winners. I am proud to have been won over by her indomitable spirit, great work ethic, and passion for the sport. I am even prouder to have been her coach.

In June 2011, I attended Ruthie's Women's Basketball Hall of Fame induction ceremony in Knoxville, Tennessee. I was very emotional when I heard her acceptance speech and how much she valued my contributions to her success.

We salute Ruthie's accomplishments and encourage her undaunted passion to help others follow in her footsteps.

Joe Ciampi, Assistant Coach
WNBA Atlanta Dream
Former Coach, Auburn University

**To my parents,
Linwood and Leola Bolton,**

**Who by example taught us
the power of faith, attitude and character.**

CHAPTER ONE
THE JOURNEY BEGINS

Whenever I speak to a group of children I begin by telling them something about my background. That way, they'll know where I came from and how I got to where I am today. It wasn't a smooth journey and one I probably could not have made if not for the things that happened in my childhood. People who don't know me are surprised to learn that I come from a family of 20 children in the tiny, rural Mississippi town of McLain. Today, McLain has fewer than 1,000 residents. That's how it all started. I was born on May 25, 1967, the 16th child of Linwood and Leola Bolton.

The Bolton Family, 1976

Just for the record, here are the names of all 20 of us: Earl, Catherine, Ceola, Linda Ruth, Linwood Jr., Betty Ann, Rose Marie, Lucille, James, Jessica, Byrone, Mary, Jerry, Paul, Maeola, Alice Ruth (that's me), Allen Ray (my twin), Nathaniel, Tanglyn and Inez. There's almost a 30 year age gap between Earl and Inez. The first thirteen were born at home and the last seven, including me, were born in a hospital. Mom was only 15 when she had her first; Dad was about 20. She adored kids and just loved being a mother. She always knew just what each cry meant from each child.

My dad moved to Mississippi from Louisiana when he was six months old. His parents had separated and he came to Mississippi with his dad, who later remarried. They moved to McLain, which was 45 miles from Mobile, Alabama. Hattiesburg, Mississippi, the home of Brett Favre, is about 25 miles away. My mom's family was living in McLain two blocks from where I grew up. Her name was Leola Hugger. My parents first met when she was 10 or 11 years old, and they were married when she was 16 and he was 22.

Dad worked at a wood shop and later as a field hand. One day he was out in the fields when he said he felt a calling for the first time. At first, he didn't think it was real, but the feeling continued to gnaw at him; something just telling him to be a minister. He later said that God called him for a purpose. He never regretted what he went through in his early life, especially dealing with a mother who didn't want him. Becoming a minister led him to accept these things. He studied very hard and eventually attended bible school in Hattiesburg and ultimately received a doctorate in Theology from the college. He began preaching while he was in his twenties. Mom left school in the eighth grade, but later returned to earn her GED. Educational opportunities were very limited in rural Mississippi at the time, especially for African-Americans.

Like many rural preachers, Dad worked at several churches. Our local church was the Mt. Gilliard Baptist Church. Many considered it to be in McLain, but the church was on the McLain-Little Creek line, maybe three or four miles from our home. We usually walked there. Dad preached at the Plymouth Rock Baptist Church in Hattiesburg. He would preach at Mt. Gilliard in the morning and Plymouth Rock in the evening. He would also travel to two churches in Louisiana, sometimes visiting people in hospitals. We often went along to support him. Sometimes he would go to Louisiana twice a month and then spend the other two weeks at the churches in Mississippi. Keeping so busy all the time was never too much for him. It was his calling and he did it willingly, without complaint.

Life in McLain

It's probably hard for some of you to realize how small a town like McLain was. There was only one main street, Highway 98, which is now called Ruthie Bolton Avenue. It is a two lane road that goes right through the center of town. In fact, you could drive through McLain in just two minutes. When I was young, there wasn't even a traffic light. Finally, they put one up, but they just left the light flashing. Now it's gone again and the reason is simple: there's almost no traffic.

The town had one hardware store and a single grocery store, both about a mile from our house. In fact, everything in the center of town was close together in about a ten block radius. The school was right there as well. We could walk everywhere. The post office was a block away from the grocery and hardware store; the laundromat across the street next to the gas station. That was the hangout spot. People came there to see friends, and watch the cars go back and forth while guessing what color the next one would be. The railroad tracks ran parallel to the road. On the way to church and Sunday school, we usually walked along the tracks. We'd always held onto each other, while looking for a train coming. The oldest sibling was always in charge of keeping us safe.

There were really no places to eat in town. Someone would set up a stand at the gas station and sell fish sometimes. Thank God for my mother and sisters; they could really cook. Eventually, there was another gas station at the other end of town by the church. When we went to church, we were always told not to go to the store inside the station. It was called Big K and had snacks, sandwiches, and Slurpees with ice cream. Some of the cups the Slurpees came in had the words "one point" printed on the side. If you got four points, you'd get a free Slurpee, so we'd always look for the cups anywhere we could find them. We would go into the trash cans looking for the Slurpee cups with points. If we found four we'd get the free Slurpee, and that was heaven to us then.

None of the stores had multiple stories. They were all just one level. The next school was 20 miles away. Many kids from the nearby towns came to McLain. There were two or three houses by the school, all of which had white people living in them. The school principal had a fine looking house right across from the school—brick home with a nice yard. All the other houses and farms were just outside of town.

My parents told me how segregation had affected them in the years past. There was only one cafe in town. Back then it was for whites only. If blacks wanted food, they had to get it through a side window; they couldn't go inside. Blacks were allowed to only use a certain area of the laundromat too. Of course, there was both a black and a white school, with the black school located out of the way down by the river. Whenever blacks went to the grocery store, they could only enter if they walked in behind a white person. Mom also told us that the Ku Klux Klan once had a presence in McLain. It started to change about the time I was born. The schools were desegregated by Supreme Court order in 1965, so I really didn't experience too much segregation; maybe just a taste of it when I was very young.

We still retained a fear of segregation during those early years. Dad would tell us to mind our own business and to use common sense. He didn't want us saying anything that could be considered offensive. That's one reason so many black people spent most of their time working in the fields and in church: it kept them away from potential trouble. There were some fights at school, a few between blacks and whites, but I don't have any recollection of raw segregation. My older sisters would tell some bad stories from their early years, like not being allowed to go into a store until a white person walked in before them. Dad helped them through it. He'd say we're not fighting them, but the negative spirits inside them. He would always tell us that there is some good in everyone, and that's what we should look for.

During the time I was growing up, the paper mill company in nearby New Augusta was the biggest company offering employment. The grocery store also offered work and one of my brothers became a butcher there. Kids made a few dollars by bagging groceries. Most of the African-Americans in McLain subsisted by working the land. There just wasn't much else there.

Our Home

We lived on a small farm of about 20 acres. One of my older sisters told me that my dad inherited the land from his father. We raised animals for food and grew vegetables in the fields. Dad also sold wood and hay, though we kept enough hay to feed our cattle. Mom made delicious jelly and jam from Mayhaw berries, which we would scoop up off the water since the trees grow in swamps and bogs. It's a berry found only in the Deep South.

Our family lived in a one story wooden house with a back porch and little else. It originally had just three rooms and was only about 800 square feet! My parents moved into it about 1945. Their first ten children were born there. At first, it only had a kitchen, a living room and one bedroom. Eventually, my parents added two more bedrooms, a bathroom and a car port. By the time there were 15 kids – though some had already left – they added another bathroom and turned the car port into another bedroom.

The Bolton Siblings inside the Old House

At first, the house didn't have running water. There was an outhouse in the back and a pump on the back porch. For years, we heated water on a wood stove for baths and to wash dishes.

When you walked into the living room there were two couches and a small television. Behind that was the kitchen, with the bedrooms in the very rear. There were always three or four of us sharing a bedroom and the entire house was set up on bricks with no basement. I remember having to dress extra warm when it got cold because we had just one little portable electric heater. One day I almost burned the house down by putting paper into the heater, trying to make it warmer. The heater started burning and a nearby curtain caught fire. One of my nephews was sitting by the heater and his face was burned a bit. He still has the scar from it. I was very saddened by what happened to him.

Life in the old house wasn't easy. I think 15 of us lived there at one time. Finally, in 1973, when I was six, my family built "the new house" constructed from bricks. This house had five bedrooms, two baths, a living room, dining room, kitchen, and wash room. It was a one-story home, and though we still had to share, it was much more comfortable than the old house. There were bunk beds for the boys and the girls shared bedrooms. My parents kept one room for guests and we weren't allowed to sleep there. There was another room for young married couples. Some of my siblings stayed there after they were married until they went out on their own.

A large field separated the new house from the old house. The old house just stayed empty for years until it was covered with weeds. It was still there after my parents passed away. Eventually, we cleaned off the area and took the house down. Maybe it was a reminder of how things used to be. Many of my brothers and sisters grew up in the old house under difficult conditions. Though the new house was larger, had running water and bathrooms, life in McLain was still harsh and we always wondered what the future would bring.

My Dad did not want our new house to ever be sold. He wanted it to be a place where the family and the grandchildren could go. There's a graveyard out in back, in one of the fields. My parents are buried there, as is my brother Paul and one of my nieces. Paul died in a car accident in November 2001. My mom passed away in 1995 and my dad in 1998. For a while we all were still in shock of losing our parents. It made it hard to stay at the house. It remained empty for many years, but finally, we cleaned it up to have a Christmas celebration there. When a house is empty it loses life. Dad always wanted it to remain part of the family because there was so much history vested in it. He wanted us to keep the house, just in case someone needed it. My sister Mary lives there now, keeps it up, and shares it with all of us.

In September of 2010, we decided we wanted to open up our land to the entire community to give back to the community that nurtured us. We built two basketball courts so family and friends can play basketball. We had a little ceremony there with the Mayor and town officials involved.

Now we're trying to obtain funding to build a community center right across from the house. I know a project like this would make my mom and dad happy. Dad always felt making a difference was important and that people should serve others. When we get approval for the community center grant, we'll be able to do that. We know that our dad would be proud of us. "A family that prays (plays) together stays together," he would fondly say.

Growing Up

I guess you could say I was always a tomboy. I loved outside chores and hard work in the fields. It always felt good to me. The inside chores, such as washing dishes and folding clothes weren't the same. Given a choice, I'd rather be outside picking the clothes off the line than inside folding them, so I would often trade jobs with one of my sisters who preferred to be inside. My sister Mary usually had the job of combing our hair. She would get mad at me because I wanted to be the last one. That way, I could stay outside longer. Even then, I always felt that if you lost a day, you would never get it back. I hated to waste a good day getting my hair done—I was only seven or eight years old at the time.

Ruthie at 8 years old

My sister Betty was my head start teacher between the ages of three and five. She told me I was the first one in my class to read. She also said I was very well behaved and very protective of my twin brother, Allen Ray. Believe it or not, I was always bigger and stronger than he was when we were younger. I was also more athletic. I was quiet then, while Allen Ray talked all the time, sometimes saying good things and sometimes not. You just couldn't get him to stop talking. My brother Nathaniel was just 13 months younger and a lot more like me. We were always very close because we liked doing the same things outside, always challenging each other and playing all kinds of competitive games.

I guess we really started having chores to do when we were about nine or ten. Mom always directed the chores and took care of the house and fields. Dad had my brothers work with the animals—hogs, horses and cows. I used to help harvest the fields and did a lot of hoeing. You had to do it right because if you didn't know how to keep the grass and weeds away from the vegetables they would take the nourishment from them. I always knew how important this was and tried to do it as well as I could. Later, I would often go out and pick peas. I wanted to do those things because I knew the more that I did, the less Mom would have to do. I always hated seeing her have to work so hard.

We kept about 10 hogs, 10 cows, some chickens and one horse at a time. My brother Paul always loved horses and would always take care of them and protect them. The cows and hogs were eventually slaughtered to provide food. I can remember the horrible sound of the hogs as they were being taken to be slaughtered. Mom had a freezer we bought from Sears and we used it to freeze a lot of meat. The animals were always outside in the field in a fenced area. We also had some outside dogs. I was afraid of the dogs. As a matter of fact, one dog's name was Snoop. One day he chased me. I was so scared, and ran so fast, I jumped over a fence and got my arm stuck in the barbed wire. I cried and cried in pain. My arm had to be stitched up. I still have the scar and for that reason, I will never forget Snoop.

There was a barn near the house that we used to store hay. Dad would pay some people to come in and roll it for us. We used an old Ford truck to bring the hay into the barn. If we ran out of hay, we had to buy it from another farmer. Thankfully, we did not run out of hay too often.

All of us helped to pick the corn. We'd all jump off the Ford truck and pick the corn from one area, then drive to another and do it again. Corn was a real staple in our lives. Mom would boil it and fry it for us, and we used it as animal feed as well. I guess we always had about 75 percent of the 20 acres planted at one time. The only things we bought were bread, sugar and milk. Occasionally, we milked the cows. We eventually had two freezers in the back room, which also held our washing machine, and we usually had enough meat to last us for a year. Rice and cornbread were cooked daily. So, for the most part, we were living off the land.

While the white to black ratio in town was about 60 to 40, white people on the whole didn't have as much land and didn't farm it as much as we did. Those who did farm had better equipment and were able to pay people to help work their land. We had an old tractor, for instance, and it would break down a lot. Sometimes we couldn't afford to get it fixed, so it would just sit until we could get the money for repairs. The white people worked the land more as a business, selling their produce, while we did it to sustain ourselves. They also sold their hay to black folks who needed it. They owned all the stores in town. I can remember having some white friends when I was young. One of my friends, in fact, was a girl named Hope. She was a very smart girl. Another friend, Debbie Smith, took pictures of my sister and me throughout high school. We are still good friends today. Dad would tell us to always be kind to people and, as a result, I was nice to everyone.

When it came to sports, I first began playing with my siblings in the backyard, maybe when I was eight or nine. In the south, children played outside all the time. We would use whatever we could find to create a game, like putting an old tire on a tree for a basketball hoop. We had a great old time just with that. One Christmas, we were given a real rim and put it on a pole with no backboard. Finally, one of my brothers built a backboard. We played so much that the grass died away and we had a flat dirt court. That's where my fondness for basketball began. I played on my first organized basketball team at school when I was 12.

My older sister, Maeola, had a strong natural talent for basketball, more than I did. It just came easily for her. She played at a very high level, both offensively and defensively. Once she became a high school star, she had coaches from 20 top colleges wanting her to come to their school and play. I was a year behind her but never felt I could come close to playing that well. But if you want to be the best, you have to play your best. Maeola became a challenge for me. I enjoyed playing with her and against her. Her high game in high school was 43 points; mine was 38. When I saw how badly the colleges wanted her, it made me want to work harder so I could get there too. We played one-on-one all the time and I finally beat her one day. When that happened, she told me I was ready for the next level.

Basketball wasn't the only sport we played when we were young. We used to play volleyball using the clothesline as the net. We did it when Mom wasn't home because she was always afraid that we'd knock it down. There were no real volleyball rules, only what we made up. We would just keep hitting the ball over the clothesline. We also created all kinds of relay races were you'd jump and run to a certain point, touch a tree and then run back. Sometimes we went out onto the street and drew a line that we had to reach, then turn and run back. If there was too much traffic that day, we would go back into the yard.

We also had sack races, jumped puddles, and climbed trees. I loved the competition and how it made me feel. I always wanted to be active and keep moving my body, and loved contact sports as a kid. I made basketball a contact sport when we played. Over time, I gradually went from just being active to participating in organized sports. Today, kids have to pay for so much of their training; back then we trained for free in the backyard. I grew up playing hard almost every day and having fun at the same time. Even in later years, working out was always fun for me, never something I dreaded. I would always train hard because I always needed to move, to do something physical all the time. In a way, it always made me feel as if I was doing something worthwhile. It all came from the way I lived as a child.

My mom's sister, Aunt Georgia, lived four or five miles away. She had 18 kids and they would come over a lot, especially in the summer. We would all play together, run up and down the road and have a good time. Between all my siblings and so many cousins, there was always something to do and plenty of people around. It was really a fun childhood.

Any discussion of childhood sports wouldn't be complete if I didn't talk about my brother Nathaniel who was 13 months younger than me. I probably looked more like Nathaniel than my twin, Allen Ray. We also had the same interests and did a lot of things together when we were young. We used to jump fences a lot, often together in unison. We would sometimes jump fences for 30 or 45 minutes at a time. We'd also see who could jump over a hole filled with water or who could do it the most times in 30 seconds. We'd climb trees to see who could go the highest or furthest out onto a limb, or even who could hang on a limb the longest. We constantly challenged each other. Nathaniel said I challenged him in a way that encouraged him. We tried to make a game out of everything we did. He was better at some things, while I was better at others. In the early years, Nathaniel would be rough and tough during the day, then would suck his thumb and turn into a baby in the evening. Sometimes before dinner he would lie down on the floor and say he wanted some ice cream. He would throw a tantrum in front of Mom, but jump right up when Dad came in. That would happen when he was about seven or eight, but after the age of ten he began to grow up. Like me, he always wanted to be outside. He sometimes got lazy with his chores, complained and cried, but he eventually learned it was his responsibility to do his share of the work. I would tell him to quit whining and just do it. Later, he didn't want me to show him up and he began to develop the same kind of competitive attitude I had. Eventually, he became an amazing athlete. He was outstanding in both football and basketball. In the end, he chose football as his primary sport.

....

🏆 *I loved the competition and how it made me feel.*

....

Playing Can Be Dangerous

Nathaniel and I played so rough sometimes that we didn't realize the danger. Climbing trees can certainly lead to an accident, as can jumping fences. I remember one time we just started throwing rocks and Nathaniel hit Allen Ray in the head with one. There was a lot of bleeding and Nathaniel got in real trouble for that one. He always liked to throw things, and Dad used to have to tell him not to throw things in the house. When I was about nine or ten, we were trying to push each other off a big sand hill, and I finally jumped off and landed on a broken bottle. I probably would have had 20 stitches, but Mom took care of it. Believe it or not, I was on homemade crutches for about two months. I was very fortunate that I didn't sever a tendon. Sure enough, after I recovered we played the same games, only I vowed not to get pushed off that hill again. We did things then that I wouldn't recommend to anyone today.

Allen Ray, my twin, was never into sports in the same way Nathaniel and I were. We still spent a lot of time together as children and often dressed alike. He was a natural born entertainer and entrepreneur. As early as the fifth grade, Allen Ray thought about ways to make money. Allen Ray and I made up a song together and would stand up on a big empty gas tank, sing and dance. Then we would jump off and do a flip. He was great at it but I would sometimes just jump down. We did this at school and the kids would watch us. Allen Ray wanted to charge every kid who was there a quarter, and while we never did, he sure talked about it a lot!

Allen Ray was into music and could sing very well. Sometimes he would try to race with me, but I was always quicker. My body makeup was stronger than his; we really were opposites as twins. He would challenge me often, but I would beat him at most athletic competitions. He was always trying to prove himself because he certainly didn't like it when I was better; it was a "boy versus girl" thing. However, he was extremely talented when it came to music. He went to a different high school, New Augusta in Beaumont, because they had a better music program. He could drum and dance, and eventually earned a music scholarship. Today, his children have a mix of both our personalities. They're shy, but very smart, and very athletic like me. When my twin and I were both young, we were very curious and would ask a lot of questions. One thing about Allen Ray, he always spoke his mind. He was never at a loss for words.

Even though Allen Ray wasn't good at basketball, he was an extremely fast runner. He would start running and then tell Nathaniel and me to try to catch him. We never said no to an opportunity to run. One time we were behind Allen Ray when he pulled on the clothesline and decided to shoot past us. The first rope missed us, but the second rope caught us and flipped us on our backs. We were very blessed to have not gotten seriously injured. My Mom wasn't happy about the situation. Allen Ray always kept teasing us that we couldn't catch him. He was right that time.

I was a good student and always got good grades. Allen Ray continuously tried to copy my work. He was slightly more book smart than I was, but was lazy at times. At some church events, we had to memorize holiday speeches. He always asked for the longest speech. I was very impressed about how much he could remember. I always wanted to get extra credit at school and I didn't want to leave room for error. I guess I was just born with a strong drive to succeed and it was nourished by my family and surroundings. My third grade teacher used to talk about how much I loved being outside yet still did all my school work. I had an English teacher in high school named Margaret Cobb who wrote a poem about my dedication to my work after I had gone to the Olympics. I always had a strong sense of responsibility and accountability. Her class was one that always stood out because she put in the time and made sure we learned. She tried teaching us to think critically and would challenge us to strive for mastery. She had a great teaching technique.

The hard work paid off later when I made the Southeastern Conference All-Academic team while I was at Auburn University. I had to study hard and found when I did this, I could get good grades. Like so many other things, my work ethic can be traced to all that happened to me when I was growing up.

As a young child, I wished I was lighter skinned. My older sister, Maeola, had a lighter complexion than I did. At that time, many African-Americans seemed to want lighter skin. I just didn't think I was pretty enough. I remember having a complex about my hair. It didn't look good to me without a ribbon in it. That's why I try to keep it so perfect today. One day when I was in the third grade, I got into trouble for playing with my hair all day. I'd take the bows off that Mom put on and then put them back again. Finally, Mom stopped putting them there, so I sneaked some in my pocket on picture day and put three or four of them on my ponytail. Mom really got mad at me that day, but it was all part of growing up.

The Bolton Family around family tractor, 1984

We obviously had a very large family, certainly larger than most. From the earliest time I can remember Dad put an emphasis on closeness, on the importance of family sticking together. "We're a unit," he used to say. "If you're going to fight someone, don't fight among yourselves. Every one of you came from the same place, but you all have different fingerprints, even the twins." If any two of us began fighting, he would stop it. We immediately had to kiss and makeup. There should always be harmony, he would tell us, and not a lot of chaos. He felt a responsibility to lead, teach and direct. He would tell us that we might not understand it all now, but he was our father and we would have to abide by his rules and laws. When we got older, he told us, we would understand.

In a large family, with big age differences between the children, the older kids were almost like second parents. They were in charge when our parents weren't home. I can remember thinking that my oldest brother was my dad because he always told me what to do. He would often say, "When I'm in charge, I'm your daddy." He would try to imitate Dad. We all learned to respect each other—the difference in age didn't matter. Even at three years old when my older sister Betty became my Head Start teacher, I knew I had to behave.

Today, everyone stays in touch and no one in our family takes anything or anyone for granted.

We have always been close and since Mom and Dad passed away, we've been closer than ever. We never thought they would leave us and in a way, they haven't—they live on through all of us. We became closer because of the legacy Dad left for us. We all felt a responsibility to pass his teachings down to the next generation. We were given the right tools and the right foundation, something I will detail in the next chapter. We want to stick together and continue to teach our family about their heritage and our family principles. All of us try to mend fences and fix what is broken. Dad taught us all the importance of forgiving and moving forward.

Dad also led many family devotions that I remember well. Between the ages of nine to eleven, I recall that we lived our lives around the church and prayed often. We were constantly in church and saw his devotion, love and passion for what he did. He truly believed deeply and practiced what he preached. Because we spent so much time at prayer meetings and choir rehearsal, we would sometimes miss functions at school. In fact, we often heard the same things at home that we heard at church. As a young girl, I sometimes got tired of hearing things repeated so much. I can remember being upset one time because I couldn't go to a school dance due to a commitment at church.

When I reached high school it all began making sense. Before, I was just a kid enjoying life. By my junior year I was mature enough to understand a bit more. My sister, Maeola, was being recruited for college basketball teams and coaches were beginning to show interest in me too. My dad began talking to me about the temptations you'll encounter in college and how to remain strong from a spiritual standpoint. So much of what he said all those years, now meant more to me than ever.

The light really came on in college. I saw negative things that so many other people were doing and the divisions within their families. When you're somewhat on your own, you have to grow up real fast. That's when I fully realized why my dad believed so strongly in the things he told us. I was excited about going to college and being away from home. Yet after a while, I couldn't wait to go home because I wanted to talk to my dad and learn even more from him. It was a way of refueling and becoming hydrated again—a way of becoming spiritually rejuvenated. That's when I totally appreciated everything my dad stood for and all the advice he had given me over the years.

All in all, I was a happy kid. Sometimes I got in trouble for laughing during our family devotions. Something would strike me as funny and I'd burst out laughing. Sometimes when I had to give a speech in church I'd begin to laugh. I often tell kids today that you may think your parents are from another planet, but they really have to be your spiritual eyes and ears. Kids often don't see a variety of potential dangers and become angry when their parents won't let them do or try something. But responsible parents are always looking out for your best interests. In my case, I was fortunate to have a mother and father who really cared and wanted to prepare us to be the best we could be in the future.

Some of my older siblings already have five or six children. I have two. We all say today that we have more respect than ever for Mom and Dad because of what they did with all their children—teaching us, disciplining us, keeping structure in the house and holding us together. That's why we had so many family devotions. I still don't know how my parents raised so many children. They always told us that family must stick together. Life throws a lot of things at people. They must learn how to deal with everything while keeping their sanity and wits about them. It's important to keep your faith in God. It's an easier thing to do when everything is going great. It becomes more difficult when there are roadblocks put up. That's when your faith is really tested.

Dad would tell us that he wouldn't be there forever. "I'll leave you with principles," he'd say, "but not a lot of money." I think we've all learned now that those principles were the most important thing he could have given us. They're still with us every single day.

This chapter should give you a very good idea about the environment in which I grew up, as well as a quick glimpse of my large family. In the following chapters, I will go into greater detail about the solid foundation I received from my parents, especially my dad, and how it has helped me with everything I have done and achieved. That foundation not only enabled me to cope with the difficulties of life, but also to become the person I am today. The advice that I will give in the coming chapters all comes from experience, from my journey, and I can only hope that it will also help you achieve your ride of a lifetime.

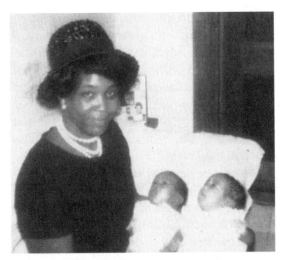

Mrs. Leola Bolton and the twins Ruthie and Allen Ray

Ruthie and twin brother, Allen Ray

CHAPTER TWO
BUILDING A FOUNDATION

There are several meanings for the word foundation. One is *the strong base from which a building is built up.* The dictionary also defines it as *the underlying principle or idea on which something is based.* I think both of these definitions apply to the foundation a person needs to develop a strong, honest and forthright character, as well as an optimistic and positive outlook on life. Coming from a family of 20 children and living in rural McLain, Mississippi, I could have been easily lost in the shuffle. Without a strong foundation my whole outlook on life might have been different. I wouldn't have had the character to work hard, the knowledge to dream big, and the desire to achieve my goals. A strong foundation is truly a base upon which to build your dreams while giving you the sound principles that allow you to achieve them.

You've got to remember that not everyone has the same kind of family situation. My family was exceptionally large, but I was fortunate enough to get so much sound advice and personal attention from my parents, especially my dad. Large or small, a stable family with two caring parents is a blessing. Even if you aren't lucky enough to have that, you shouldn't give up. There are other ways to build a strong foundation and people who can help you achieve it. What is important is that you realize this can be done and that you are someone special. Helping you to do this is one of the reasons I'm sharing my life and the things I've learned with you. Building a strong foundation, then, can happen in a number of ways. Here's how it happened with me.

With 20 children, my mom always had a great deal of work to do. She loved us all. I guess she really must have loved children in general to have had so many. When I was born in 1967 my older brother, Earl, was 25 and already out on his own. I don't remember him actually living with us. There were probably three or four children out of the house as I was growing up. There were always at least eleven at home at one time. With grandchildren already coming, we always seemed to have about 20 there at once.

Ruthie and family at the Women's Basketball Hall of Fame Induction Ceremony, June 2011

My mom was good with all the kids. Sometimes there were babies crying and making noise, and kids running around everywhere. To someone walking in the door for the first time, it probably looked like a daycare center. Mom knew just what to do in any situation. Besides taking care of the younger ones, she cooked and washed clothes. She was busy all the time with one thing or another. She'd sometimes ask for help folding clothes. If she didn't want to help, she wouldn't say anything and do it herself, but I always helped her whether she asked me or not. I knew how hard she worked and how much she always had to do. I enjoyed helping out to lessen her workload. In fact, when I was old enough, I would get up early and go out in the fields with her to tend the gardens and gather vegetables for dinner. When I left for college I remember she said that her only dependable helper was leaving her. I chose to be a responsible helper at a young age and that helped me become a reliable team player.

Mom was an expert cook. Like a master chef, she could bake breads and cakes without measuring. She made it a point to share her knowledge of cooking with me or any of the girls who wanted to learn. Despite all the children and the work she was always active. She sang as she cleaned the house, usually old southern spiritual songs or soothing hymns that connected with God: *Amazing Grace* and *Precious Lord*. She was also a woman who always wanted to look good and would never go out with rollers in her hair or with anything that would make her look less than her best. When she walked into church Dad would say, "*This is my wife; doesn't she look good!*" Mom was always embarrassed when he said things like that, but it showed just how proud he was of her.

Linwood and Leola Bolton

Mom would often say, "Thank God for my husband and for my 20 kids. I love them all because I just have love in my heart." That was Mom, talking about love. In fact, she couldn't understand how people couldn't love each other. So much of my love for people has come from my mom and that is definitely part of the solid foundation I received. Though my dad was the leader of the family, I know that behind every great man there's an even greater woman. They didn't have a perfect marriage. No one does. They had their disagreements, but always about small, minor things. They also had different likes and dislikes, but the most important thing was their spiritual chemistry. In spirituality, they were one, and their objective was to raise the family the way God wanted them raised. This was their foundation: true love and true unity. Their positive role modeling strengthened my foundation and desire to be a strong support for others.

Rev. Linwood Bolton, Foundation Builder

My dad was a man I looked up to in many ways. He was the most influential person in my life, defining the way I chose to live. He wasn't a big man, standing about five-foot-seven and weighing 150 pounds with a very small frame. He always dressed like a preacher with his hat on his head. He was a calm man who didn't scream and was never angry or frustrated. I can't remember him ever raising his voice to any of us. He felt so strongly about speaking in a calm voice to loved ones, that he would even ask his own siblings, "Why do you raise your voice to your children? Give your command and move on." He was always ready to talk if someone needed him or if he felt he had something to say to any or all of us.

....

> 🌐 *"If you take with you in life just a few principles,*
> *you won't have to carry a suitcase full of rules."*
> *— Rev. Linwood Bolton*

....

My dad had a great enthusiasm for life. He said that every person has a choice on how he embraces each day—and his choice was to work hard. If you asked him how he felt, he always told you he felt great! "If I choose to be sad," he would say, "I could complain about my back hurting, but what will that do for my day? I just want to live my life happy with peace and joy." The man was continuously upbeat. His entire mentality was about having a positive attitude. If you broke a leg, he'd say, "You still have to look on the positive side. You could have broken two." I've always been thankful to have a dad who had such a zest for life. It fed my positive attitude.

He wanted to get inside our souls and into the depths of our hearts. He became a part of us and we soon came to realize how important it was to have that positive attitude, especially in today's world. Dad would say, "You can't worry about other people's perspectives, but you can change your response to it." That was the key. How you deal with any adverse situation is determined simply by your approach to it. Many of the decisions I have made in my life were guided directly by his advice.

For example, I wasn't one of the primary 50 players invited to try out for the United States National Basketball Team in 1995. The implication—I simply wasn't good enough. The only alternative I had was to pay my own way to the tryouts, which would cost $600. My coaches at the time, as well as some others, told me I'd be wasting my money. They thought I didn't have a chance. But Dad told me it was my choice. Then he said, "If you don't go, you may have to live with your own regret and wonder what would have happened. The worse thing that can happen is you don't make the team, but at least you tried and pursued your passion." I took Dad's advice, paid my own way and made the team. They even returned my $600. Thanks to Dad, I always keep a positive attitude and approach everything with that frame of mind. But he didn't stop there.

Dad called family devotions often. Whenever Dad felt there was a message to share he would gather us all together, whether it was the middle of the day or at midnight. No matter what you were doing at the time, he wanted your total attention. If there was a guest in the house that person could either stay or leave during the family devotions. During his devotions, there were absolutely no distractions. This meant no television, no cooking on the stove, no one talking or kidding around. He told that to Mom, too. He wanted these sessions to be total devotions. That's how much they meant to him.

Dad never told anyone to go. A devotion might last just 10 minutes but he always had a topic to discuss, something that would teach us a lesson about life. For example, when he saw something on the news about a domestic disturbance, problems within a family, he would talk about that. He would stress the importance of peace within the family and how fighting leads to bad consequences. He would talk about how so many people hurt the ones they love instead of thinking of ways to help them. One time, we were playing all day with our cousins when we suddenly decided to fight them. Dad found out and gave 10 of us whippings, one after another. That's how much fighting upset him.

He would always finish his devotions by citing a couple of bible passages: John 3:16 or Psalms 23. Sometimes he talked about Cain and Abel, again emphasizing family unity and togetherness. He usually wanted us to hear some quotes—things that he hoped would stay with us. One of his favorites was, "If you take with you in life just a few principles, you won't have to carry a suitcase full of rules." He would also say, "You know about me. I'm a man of principles, a man of dignity. I don't care a lot about the hoop-la. I say what I mean and mean what I say." In other words, he was telling us that he didn't go around with a chip on his shoulder and wasn't impressed by a lot of material things. He didn't need to have the best. It meant more to him to be a good dad doing the right thing. He never went out of his way to impress people and keep up with the Joneses. He would say, "I don't have time for that."

Everything with my dad was about family and about sticking together. He would tell us that there will always be things that can divide a family, such as jealousy, and that we should avoid falling into that trap. Fighting in the home was forbidden. He reminded everyone that people are given a name for a reason. He insisted we call our siblings by their correct name. He admitted that he and our mom had their conflicts and sometimes criticized each other, but at the end of the day, both of them knew that their relationship was based on love. That was never a question, and he explained that even their confrontations occurred in a loving and kind way. More than anything, Dad was solid. He would say, "If you have a watch that says 10:02 and someone says it's 10 o'clock, and you change it, then an hour later do the same thing, and you'll find yourself changing it again, over and over." In other words, you'll be doing things that other people tell you to do. Some people can't stick to their own rules and principles, and change too much to please other people. He wanted us to be solid in what we believed and to remain grounded.

With his solid beliefs and principles, it shouldn't be surprising that my dad had such a profound influence on my life from the time I was a little girl right up to the day he died. He gave me so much that's it's hard to know where to begin. What I do know, however, is that when all was said and done, he had given me the best foundation a person could have. That foundation has stayed with me through thick and thin, and has allowed me to pursue my goals and dreams without fear of failure. I can't emphasize enough how very important that is.

These are a few of the basic fundamentals of his philosophy. For starters, he would always tell us that he chose to live his life happy. Sure, there were times when certain things would make him unhappy, but he always said that an individual has a choice about how he or she wants to embrace each and every day. If you don't exercise that choice, your day will do it for you. His choice was to be happy and his goal was to always be joyful. He felt that joy was a constant, while happiness would sometimes come and go. Joy, he said, can be with you through sad and disappointing moments, and that's what sustains your soul – pure joy and peace in the midst of any storm.

....

✺ *Three things that determine what a person becomes:*

1) Attitude
2) Motive
3) Character

....

He would tell us that there are three things that sum up an individual and determine what a person becomes. They are: 1) attitude; 2) motive; and 3) character. These are the qualities that determine whether you will be good or bad. Some people certainly have a bad attitude, the wrong motives, and a poor character. He didn't want that for any of us. To illustrate this, he would compare a character to a picture. You may not like everything in the picture, such as the way your hair looks, but that picture is you. In the same way, your character is who you are. Then you have to ask, *What do I want my character to look like to other people?* In the end, it's up to you to decide what kind of character you want. That's your DNA makeup, and everything comes back to attitude and to your frame of mind.

A large part of building character is making the right decisions. Dad would say, "If the Devil has your mind then he's got you sewed up in his watch-pocket and you can't get out." He meant that you can't let someone control your thoughts or your mind. You must be in control at all times and be responsible for your own decisions. He gave us this example: "Say I have a bird in my hand behind my back and ask you if you think the bird is dead or alive. If you say it's alive I can kill it behind my back. If you say it's dead, I can let it go and be free. I'm controlling you in that situation. You have to be in control of your decisions."

He didn't want us to live our lives with resentment. If you look back and realize you made a mistake, let it be. You made it. If you're blaming everyone else for what happens to you then you're setting yourself up for a stressful life. You're giving other people too much control, forgetting that only you can make your own improvements. Always keep moving forward and looking ahead to the new day.

Another part of character, he told us, is learning to forgive. In fact, my dad called the ability to forgive one of life's greatest gifts. He would tell us that people with a lot of pride don't know how to forgive, and that is yet another thing that will keep them from living a joyful life. When you have that kind of pride, it's always all about you. He insisted that you forgive people with whom you're angry and even people you don't like. He would say, "Forgiving is giving up your pride." But even when you are a victim, you have to forgive. Otherwise, it will tear away at you. He felt that it's often part of human nature to become selfish. Because of this, people hesitate to say they're sorry because it makes them feel weak. But if you truly have forgiveness in your heart you'll be a better person for it and open yourself up to more possibilities and blessings.

🌸 *My Dad called the ability to forgive one of life's greatest gifts.*

A Few Rules to Live By

Everyone needs a few rules, especially when you're young and impressionable. Without rules and a strong hand to enforce them, you can fall victim to bad outside influences or simply feel that you can do as you please. A set of fair and reasonable rules that are consistently adhered to is an important part of the foundation that will make you a better person. Even though my dad believed in the need for strong principles to direct our lives, he gave us a few rules to follow to promote peace, harmony, and productivity at home. For example, whenever he spoke, we all knew we had better listen.

Dad let it be known early that he absolutely would not negotiate with his children, though he always made sure we knew that he loved all of us the same. If I brought home an A on a test and my brother brought home a D, I might get a reward, but it didn't mean he loved my brother any less. My dad would reward us based on our individual accomplishments. Another rule we had revolved around our meal time. If we had chicken for dinner, that's what you ate. You didn't complain that you didn't like it and ask for something else. If you were supposed to stay home and babysit, that's what you did. No excuses, his terms were non-negotiable.

He knew that one day, as we got older, we would eventually understand his reasoning. We knew that when we became parents, we would finally realize why he made these rules and enforced them. For example, if there was a party we wanted to attend that wasn't a mandatory school event, he usually said no. He felt that he couldn't worry about all of us and that too many potentially bad things could happen beyond his control. "If you don't go to the party," he would say, "then I don't have to give you more rules." It was important that we respected his authority and decisions. Along with everything else, it taught us basic respect for each other. Though Dad made most of the rules, he and Mom always agreed on what we had to do. Here are some of Dad's primary rules:

1. You always loved your brothers and sisters and were kind to each other. That was the most important thing. Home was a place of peace. Dad felt it was important to keep the family morale high.

2. There would be no fighting or name-calling among his children. That was a serious no-no and if it happened he would change his entire agenda to reprimand us. He felt that home should be a place of unity and love. It was all part of the family sticking together.

3. There was no horseplay, especially the kind where someone could get hurt. Dad didn't even like it when he saw a parent playfully throw a child in the air and catch him. He felt that one mistake could seriously injure or even paralyze the child. He always told the older kids not to mess with the younger ones.

4. You had complete respect for your elders and never disrespected authority. We never thought about talking back to Dad or protesting a command that Mom gave us. He didn't want to hear any arguments because that was disrespectful.

5. Because we knew he wouldn't negotiate, we never challenged him.

6. You couldn't sit in a car with a boy. This was his rule for the girls when we got older. If a friend came by, we had to bring him into the house. Dad would say, "If they don't want to come in, then they would have to leave." And if my dad hadn't met him, my friend wasn't allowed to be inside

the house while he was away. At the time, I wondered what the big deal was. Now I really do understand my dad's rule.

7. Everyone had chores to do. They were part of learning responsibility. Mom usually set up the chores and put them in writing. The girls had to wash dishes and make sure the house was clean. The boys had to make sure the hogs and cows were fed. There would be repercussions if we didn't do our chores. Sometimes you had a choice to clean up the house or work in the fields. I always chose the fields because I enjoyed the work and loved being outdoors. That was my comfort zone.

Dad may have been a bit overprotective, but that's the southern way. If any extracurricular activities weren't mandatory, we weren't allowed to do it. It could have been something like a school party. If there was a game followed by a party, we had to come home right after the game. He knew what teenagers generally liked to do and he didn't want us tempted. Remember, Dad and Mom had a lot of children to worry about. They felt there was always a church activity for us. Or, we could create games at home. You were safe, they reasoned, if you developed activities within the family community. Dad also felt you should not feel sorry for yourself if something bad happens. It isn't the end of the world and you can always find something positive in the experience. There was no time in your life for pity parties. He simply didn't want us feeling sorry for ourselves over anything. You picked yourself up and made the situation better.

We had to go to Sunday School before church. You almost had to be in the hospital to miss it! Sunday School was always mandatory. When we were kids, he didn't expect us to understand everything. He would tell us that we were trying to get to a place where he's already been. "*If you're drinking baby's milk you won't know how to digest a steak,*" was the way he put it. Then he'd add, "When you reach a certain age, you can discuss certain things with me." He was trying to let us know that he was the authority and that, as kids, we just weren't ready to understand some things. We certainly didn't understand the need for all the rules then or why he was so rigid about enforcing them. But, as we got older, we realized that everything he did had a purpose. Some of us, of course, had to learn the hard way.

Let's face it, as kids we all push the envelope and try to get away with something at one time or another. Dad was a kid once and understood why we would try to beat the system. "In my household you respect the rules." He would say, "You may not like it, but you have to respect it." I remember at the age of 16 or 17 one of my sisters quit following all the rules. My dad told her, flat out, "If you insist on going against my rules you'll have to move out." This was his version of tough love. Well, she moved out and married at a very early age. She made her decision and, fortunately, it worked out in the long run. She had 10 children of her own, all very smart. But she admits now that she lost a number of the best years of her youth. She would have loved to have dated more and gone to college. Because of her solid foundation and strong belief in herself, she beat the odds and became a kindergarten teacher. Given the chance to do it all over again, she wouldn't have been in such a hurry to grow up!

As siblings now, we all understand just where our dad was coming from. Dad's guidance helped us to make fewer mistakes. There were times when I thought he was being too strict, but now I understand that he had a reason for his rules and that each and every one was designed to protect us. I remember coming home during my sophomore year in college. I wanted to go to the movies with this guy I had met two or three weeks before. Dad said he didn't think I'd known him long enough and preferred if we went to a local football game instead. Dad felt it was a little too soon for me to go to the movies with a guy who hadn't even come into our home. Later, I discovered the guy was married, and again appreciated my dad's protection. In his own subtle way, he was a wise philosopher and teacher rather than a strict boss. I learned to respect authority and appreciate his wisdom to make my life better.

The Goodness in Everyone

As part of Dad's positive outlook, he practiced seeing the good in all people. He would tell us that if we didn't have something positive to say about someone not to say anything at all. He urged us not be too quick to judge others. "Always try to find something positive in people and feel that they all have good intentions," he would say. God created all of us, so I always allow someone to prove to me that they don't have good intentions. You can't go around thinking people are bad. That isn't good for you.

You are somebody. It may be a difficult thing to embrace the given state of the world, but Dad always lived by his philosophy. If we were watching the news and there was a story about a guy going to jail for 30 years as punishment for a terrible crime, he would still insist that there was good in that person. He just hadn't discovered it yet. To that end, Dad would tell us that we were special—that there is good in everyone. Always tell yourself, *I'm somebody*. "If you don't think it," he would tell us, "why would anyone else say or think it? Each person has his or her own unique fingerprint. You are special."

He helped me greatly by giving me this knowledge. Strangely enough, when I was young, I always had trouble spelling the word special. I learned it by using my dad's philosophy and thinking that *I am special*. By saying that, it reminded me that the "i" came before the "a." S-P-E-C-I-A-L. I share that with kids today as a way to remember that they're special. In fact, you can help your friends or family members by telling them they are special and that there is something unique about them. This is something I've done very often over the years—one more good habit I got from my dad. That wasn't all.

Dad would say, "Nothing goes on your record but what you put on it. Someone else's perspective of you doesn't matter. If you're true to yourself, you'll know how you have to grow to become better. You have to remember that, no matter what, you're still somebody and you were created for a reason. If you're not true to yourself about your own shortcomings, then you're fooling yourself. It's up to you to address who you are, not let others label you. If people say unflattering things about you, you have to answer. Silence means you're agreeing with them. Tell them you don't agree. In your own mind you must always think, "*I know who I am and I know I'm a good person.*" Too many kids today are told that they aren't going to amount to anything. If they hear it enough they may begin to believe it. So, you always have to tell yourself that you *are* somebody special, no matter what other people say.

Another point Dad emphasized was the need to be kind to others. He would sometimes point his finger and say, "I don't care how much of a Christian you are, you have to learn to deal with people. Some will make this very difficult, and difficult to love them." He would explain how it was necessary to allow for human error. "If you're going through a supermarket," he'd say, "and you run into someone having a bad day, that person may begin to yell and be confrontational." His advice was not to be too quick to react. Instead of snapping back at them, give them love and kindness in return. "You can do a great deal with kindness," he would say. He followed what the Lord said, especially the familiar bible reference to Jeremiah 31:3, "I have loved thee with an everlasting love: therefore with loving kindness, have I drawn thee." Be a peacemaker and that becomes another part of your character. It makes you a better person and allows you to enjoy life more.

My dad's ability to embody a peacemaker was something that remains a strong hold that I cling to as a reminder of how I must live and act. I don't think I've ever really had a fight with anyone since I've left home. His advice has always helped me deal with confrontation. Whenever someone does something to try to make me react badly, I think about his saying, "Deal with it, but don't do something you'll regret." This advice has helped me with teammates and coaches during my basketball days. For that reason, I think I've been considered very easy to coach. I just don't like confrontation or friction too much. I considered myself a quiet leader, leading by example. If I saw my teammates having a confrontation, I would step in and ask them what was happening. My advice was always the same. I'd suggest that they talk to each other and work it out. It's important for the team and it makes life easier. As my dad said, "Being a peacemaker keeps your own morale up."

Looking back, I can think of many situations that could have turned out badly if I hadn't turned the other cheek. I've had teammates who have said things to hurt me and I would always bite my tongue, even though I felt tears coming. I never allowed myself to stoop to their level. Instead, I would be the bigger person and walk away. Afterwards, I prayed for whoever was trying to get me to react. If I had fought them, I would have lost respect for myself. By walking away, they eventually had more respect for me. Sure, there were times when my instinct was to fight, but then I'd think about Dad and hear him asking, "What will fighting solve?" In that respect, my dad gave me that extra bit of grace. It keeps me from ever going overboard. Dad said, "There may be times when you'll shed some tears because you really want to fight, but when you think about what I've taught you, you'll settle down instead of just reacting. If you retaliate, you give the other person all the control." In just that one way, Dad's advice has helped me so much.

....

🌼 *Life is 10% what happens to you and 90% how you respond to it.*

....

How you deal with adversity and difficult situations is another way to become a good person. If you take life by the horns, then you're in control. When life overwhelms you, then you will surely suffocate under its many pressures. Dad told us we were all given minds so that we could make decisions. If someone cusses at you and you choose to cuss back, he warned us that your entire day could be ruined by that one incident. And if that happened, you couldn't blame the other person because you allowed yourself to be manipulated. How you respond to situations is a huge part of how you'll end up as a human being. Dad made it crystal clear when he said, *"Life is 10 percent what happens to you and 90 percent how you respond to it!"*

Another Way to Fight Back

In high school there was a girl who used to bully me all the time. She was nice to others but seemed bent on trying to make me fight. It reached a point where she would even put a fist in my face and threaten to hit me. My friends would ask why I was letting her do this and telling me I shouldn't let her walk all over me like that. This went on for several months. Finally, I just said to her one day when she was threatening me again, "Gladys, I'm tired of you talking to me this way. I've always been kind to you and I'm just not going to take it anymore." As soon as I said that she apologized, telling me she just wanted to be my friend, only didn't know how to come out and say it. I forgave her immediately and from that moment on, we became good friends. While you don't have to fight, you can certainly express what's on your mind and let a person know that it isn't right to treat you a certain way.

The important question to ask, as you're about to react to any situation is: "*How can this make me a better person?*" Much of your reaction comes back to the foundation you received. That's not to say you won't make mistakes. Dad would say, "As the leader of the family, my responsibility is to lay a foundation. I can't decide what you do with it when you're grown. But hopefully it is embedded in your heart and soul. If you go astray, a solid foundation may help you to find your way back."

Nathaniel, Ruthie and Charles Hartfield

That's what happened with my younger brother, Nathaniel. He was a good football player at Mississippi College. He actually had some try outs with a couple of NFL teams and the Atlanta Falcons twice, coming close to making it. After that didn't work out, he played four years in Germany with the World Football League. Then he was injured, tearing the anterior cruciate ligament in his knee. It ended his football career and he had a difficult time accepting that. He wanted to make it to the NFL and buy Mom her dream home, so the injury was devastating to him. Shortly afterward, Mom passed away and he felt he never had the chance to show how much he loved her. His answer was to mask his pain with drugs. When that happened, my dad said that he didn't regret anything he had done in raising him and that Nathaniel always had a place at home, but he wouldn't go out looking for Nathaniel every night when he didn't come home. "I've raised him for 18 years," he said, "but there's a time when he has to make his own decisions." "Experience," he repeated to us, "is the greatest teacher, if you let it work for you."

Well, it took a while, but my brother finally rediscovered his roots and the foundation he was given. He's a minister now and we often sit and talk about how the guidance we received from our dad helped him find his way again. As Dad told us, "I'll marry you; I'll counsel you; I'll give you advice. But it's ultimately your decision to choose who you want to walk down the aisle with." When we had our own families, he never interfered. But if he saw something he didn't like he would say something, and offer his advice.

My Talks with Dad

Going up to my dad's study and talking with him one-on-one remains a big part of my life. I found what he had to say was informative and educational. It gave me a great deal of comfort just to sit and speak with him. He inspired confidence in me and reinforced the great foundation he provided, making sure I remained focused and confident with a positive approach to everything I did or tried to do. No matter how tough a situation may get, my dad says, "There is always a way out."

Dad's room was loaded with books. They were everywhere. They were on shelves, his desk, alongside his chair. He read constantly and had a doctorate in theology. He believed in education and loved to teach. He always had a jar full of peppermint candy which he said helped his voice. I'll never forget the smell of sweet peppermint that filled the room. Every time I went into the room, two bibles were piled on his bed and two more were scattered on the floor by his chair. His jacket always hung lazily over his chair, as if he intended never to leave his study and camp there overnight. He only had time for philosophical articles or biblical stories. Digesting words meant far more to him than staying up to watch a television show. In fact, the only television he would watch was the news, sermons, and occasionally boxing or wrestling.

Now it is no wonder the word of God had a direct helping hand guiding my own life and my dad's life. These words came to life when I listened to my dad's sermons at church, when my dad lectured our family, but mostly, these words held value and true meaning when I could talk to my dad one-on-one about his devotions and perspective on life. When I visited my dad's study, I first asked what he had planned for the day. This brought me closer to him and I held such high admiration for him. Then, I moved on to the bigger questions and his answers were simple: "Daughter, I plan to outline my sermon today and then enjoy some of your mother's fine cooking." I asked him about the devotion he had for us the night before, trying to clarify what he meant. He was always happy when I would ask, telling me, "A lot of things come to me from experience and you will learn them." Sometimes he would be watching a sermon on TV when I went to see him. He always recorded them. I would sit quietly, admiring his dedicated eyes fixed on the television screen. I was too eager to ask him if everything the preacher said was true. Naturally, I had to wait until the preacher finished and the sermon was over. Then my dad's attention was all mine, and I could bombard him with more questions. But his response was always a simple one, no matter how many questions I would ask. He would emphasize that it was best to take only one or two things from the sermon I heard, and that it would help me.

"You've got to look at life as a buffet," he'd explain. "You can learn from almost anyone by listening and taking something from what they said. It doesn't mean everything they say is true." That's why he would say, "Life is like a buffet. You take what you want until you're satisfied."

I went into Dad's study often because I liked being in his presence. I knew he would tell me something that would help me with life. He would routinely say something profound. Even while I was in college I always wanted to go home so I could talk to my dad, if only to hear his voice. He had a calming effect on me and put me at ease. When I spoke with him he never failed to say something that cleared my mind.

Now that he's gone, I miss him profoundly. It wasn't only the tremendous foundation he gave to me, but it was also his counsel, his willingness to talk and give me his advice. Whenever I have a crisis in my life now, or even a decision to make, I think of my dad and his lessons. For all these reasons, my dad will always have a great influence on my life and will always be with me.

Ruthie and Dad, 1996

I'll never forget one miraculous experience we shared. I was concerned that his late nights would one day catch up with him. His early morning drives to different churches seemed to be an accident waiting to happen. His eyelids would close slowly and with both hands on the wheel, he transformed into a blind man driving under the starlight of an angel or the will of God. Just like his office, bibles were scattered all around the inside of the car; bibles amassed on the backseat, under his front seat, and in his trunk. But I wondered why he needed so many bibles in the car. One morning, my young quizzical thoughts found their answer. My dad slipped into his blind-man state, driving in a coma, somehow miraculously steering the wheel perfectly straight once again, waking only to mumble, "Daughter, I just had a dream about you." *What? How could my dad already be dreaming while driving?* Before I knew it, we were hit by an 18 wheeler truck and bibles went flying! The front windshield shattered and glass decorated the ground like confetti. All I could remember was seeing the huge truck come right at me and closing my eyes! Next thing I knew, I could barely hear the faint sounds of my dad, sister Ree, and Charles Hartfield calling my name. It took twenty minutes for my dad to find me. I was lying perfectly unharmed in a ditch off the side of the road, with one of Dad's bibles unexpectedly resting on my arm. I'll never forget those bibles in his car were placed there for well-intended reasons. I have pure faith that God was indeed watching us that night and the starlight of God's angels saved us, knowing we had many more days on this beautiful earth to come.

Summing Up

A strong foundation holds the building blocks of your character in place. I was blessed to have had my parents, who were able to provide a solid foundation for me that improved my ability to handle life's challenges. But if you feel you aren't getting the proper guidance at home, there are others who can help you strengthen your foundation. It might be a teacher, a relative, a coach, a clergyman or a counselor. It should be someone you trust and respect as a person; someone you admire and look up to for his or her accomplishments and solid personality. You can always benefit from the experience of someone older, someone who wants to help guide you along the proper path.

Here, are some important building blocks for a solid foundation. Each one is necessary for you to become the best person you can possibly be.

1. Always be happy and joyful with a zest for life.
2. Keep a positive attitude in everything you do.
3. Never abandon your principles.
4. Stay in control of all your decisions and don't be manipulated by others.
5. Don't blame others for your mistakes.
6. Always respect your elders.

7. Never feel sorry for yourself.
8. Be forgiving in any situation.
9. Always look for the good in all people.
10. Be a peacemaker in any confrontation.
11. Take responsibility for all your actions.
12. Treat everyone with kindness, even those who aren't always nice to you.
13. And always…always remember that you are SPECIAL.

All of these elements make up your total character and will allow you to be anything you want, as well as a person others will come to admire. Your foundation will make you strong and free to pursue all your dreams and to take that flight you once doubted or feared. Wherever you find your foundation, you should know that you deserve to make the most of it. Make it special because you *are* special—make it support the *ride of your life*!

All the Bolton Sisters and Dad

The Bolton Brothers

CHAPTER THREE
BEGINNING TO DREAM

Everybody has the ability to dream. A dream, however, is like a fantasy. You can dream about something, but if you really want to make it happen, you have to work hard. Hard work is real. You can dream every day, even if it's just about having another opportunity to jump that fence or climb another tree. In my mind, it's priceless just to have the ability to dream and then to make it happen by pursuing that dream with hard work and perseverance.

When I was very young my dreams were limited to my immediate environment. I looked forward to climbing trees, having relay races with my sisters, brothers and cousins, and taking on the next challenge. Every day I would dream about embracing a new challenge and doing better than the day before.

When I was 12, I picked cucumbers as a way of earning money. A truck would come for us early in the morning and if you missed it, you didn't go. They gave us two huge buckets to fill in one day. My brother Paul was great at it and he would show me his strategy. He moved fast. After he reached his goal of two or even three buckets, he would help us. Right away I dreamed about doing it as well as he did and I always asked him for tips so I could improve. He would tell me that the first hour is the most important; once it got hot you would begin to tire and slow down.

He also said "You don't have time to sit and eat lunch; you have to eat on the go." One day I forgot my gloves and had to use my socks as gloves. Paul would remind me that you have to be equipped, in other words, time is money. He had a good business mind and was highly organized. We were paid five dollars a bucket. If you filled two you were doing well, but Paul often filled three or four. I'd say there were about 300 or 400 cucumbers to a bucket. Soon, I began to increase my number of collected buckets, and really felt accomplished. More so, I was truly proud when my brother complimented me. Before long we were working so hard and fast that the cucumbers we picked ended up as our lunch.

So my early dreams were always short-term. For this reason, I didn't look too far ahead. I was thinking of that day and the next day. I was constantly focused on the now: doing things the right way and getting better at everything I did. Looking back, I think that was when the leader inside of me began to emerge. The things I dreamed about back when I was an eager excited child all constituted my world. You may live in a totally different world but that doesn't mean you can't have similar dreams. Because there were so many of us and our family didn't have a lot of money, I rarely dreamed about getting personal possessions. There is nothing wrong with possessions. Nevertheless, you should always try to earn them. My world taught me a lot about hard work and it didn't take long to realize that hard work was the key to making dreams come true.

Our world then was our home, school and church. I didn't see that there was a much larger world out there. Nevertheless, I took full advantage of what I had. I didn't worry about what I didn't have. In other words, I lived fully in my world and that helped to get me ready for the next stage. No matter where you live or what your situation is like, you have to find a way to make the most of your surroundings. Grow where you are. That's probably the best way to put it. I learned just what hard work was within my environment and learned from the people around me. I was never too proud to ask for help because I always wanted to be better. And, as a bonus, growing up in a large family helped me later become an effective part of a team.

There's a reason why you are where you are. You should never forget that there is always something that can be learned at this time in your life. What you learn from your immediate environment will help you in the future—help you become what you want to be. Some places are not as glamorous as others, but you've got to take advantage of the place you're in, no matter the situation.

Obviously, those early dreams do mean something. They prepare you to work hard and become a better person. When you realize that you can make your early dreams come true you won't be overwhelmed when your world expands and dreams become bigger. Learn the formula for success and betterment early, and it will always serve you well.

Some Rules For Those Early Dreams

It's important to be able to dream early, but you've got to learn quickly that it takes hard work to make all dreams come true—both the small and the larger ones that will follow. As with other things, what you learn early will carry over and help you later. There are a few rules you should know so that those early dreams aren't easily derailed. If they are, you may stop dreaming and that can only hurt you as you grow. Take a look at the following components of my success formula.

1. Education is important. Growing up, we couldn't miss school. When it came to education, Dad wouldn't allow us to goof off at all. He emphasized the value of reading and told us that education was like power. "You won't use everything you learn," he'd say, "but it will teach you to be responsible, have structure and set goals." The important thing is how you learn. Beginning to dream is part of the process, because if you dream of being the best you can be, it should begin with being the best you can be at school. If you do the best you can from the time you start school, your good habits will carry over to everything else you do and help you make all your dreams come true.

2. Put your dreams on paper. You'll learn early how to take notes in school. This is also important when you begin to dream. When you write down your dreams you'll see them more clearly. You won't just wake up and find that your dreams have come true. Start the process by describing your dreams on paper. Then you can think about ways to put each dream into action.

3. Don't keep your dreams to yourself. As with so many other things, it's always good to talk about your dreams with someone. By talking, you give the dream a foundation and you become accountable. If someone dreams of losing a certain amount of weight and they tell someone about it, that person can remind them to take positive actions to achieve that goal. In a way, it's like peer pressure—the good kind. Pick someone who you know will listen and take you seriously. It will also help you to believe in yourself. Sharing your dreams with the right people will lead to encouragement, something everyone needs. Your parents may be able to advise you about ways to achieve your dream. Other adults can offer you some words of wisdom also.

4. Deal with your naysayers. This is another reason to write down your dreams. Whenever you want something and develop a passion for it, someone will surely criticize you. It doesn't matter why people are criticizing you. The point is you must learn to let that criticism motivate you. When you're young it's sometimes difficult to handle naysayers and critics. The best way to deal with it is to talk with people who give you positive energy. These are the kind of people to stay around. Hopefully, it begins with your parents, but it can also be a relative, teacher, clergyman, coach or a good friend. Make sure you stay passionate. That's the best way to exceed expectations.

5. Pursue your early dreams. One of the beauties of dreaming at an early age is that you can dream about something one day, and then change your mind the next. You can have all these different ideas because, in many ways, dreams are simply ideas. When you're young you can think about a number of opportunities, and then pick and choose later. You have a free will to explore. At the same time work hard on your existing tasks like getting good grades at school. Then you will be ready to pursue bigger dreams.

6. Keep your dreams within reach. If you don't have a big dream now, that's okay. There's no rush. Concentrate on your attitude and your work ethic at school or at work. Get the small things in order first. Do your homework, be obedient and be accountable. I knew I had to take care of first things first. Whatever I did, I tried to do it better than the time before. If you work on your small dreams, it prepares you for those larger dreams to come. It's certainly important to dream big, but you've also got to be realistic. Dreams—which become goals—that are set too high can lead to discouragement. When you're young, keep the dreams simple and within reach. Celebrate your success in accomplishing your goal. You'll know when it's time to take it up a notch and you'll be ready to do it. Keep climbing your ladder of success—one small goal at a time.

7. Don't fear your dreams. Many kids often go through a phase where they have no fear. I was that way as a youngster—climbing trees, jumping fences and taking on all challenges. Having some fear, however, is not a bad thing. It can keep you from going one step too far and will also teach you something about yourself. It's like learning to swim for the first time. You're afraid to take that first plunge because you know you can drown. That's when you ask for help and encouragement. It's the same with dreams. If you fear them, they won't happen. But if you follow the principles outlined above, write them down, seek encouragement and work hard, you'll overcome that fear and begin to make your dreams a reality.

8. Keep your dream alive. The advice here is simple. Keep moving forward toward making that dream happen. Do things over and over again if you must, even if you fail the first time. Don't lose hold of your dream. If you're passionate about your dream, and know that it's within reach, you must continue to work hard and keep trying. Do not let the negativity, temporary failures and naysayers win. Persevere and you will make it happen.

Hope Bolton, Ruthie's daughter

Dreams Grow Up Too

When I first began to dream beyond McLain and our daily life there, I was a sophomore or junior in high school. That's when the colleges began recruiting my older sister, Maeola, for their basketball programs and she began traveling to visit various schools. Up until then, basketball had just been something that we played for fun. Yet I knew there was a yearning fire in me that kept pushing me forward. I was passionate about playing basketball. I was now more compelled to make myself a stronger and faster player. I began playing at age 9 and was on my first real team at the age of 12. When I was 13, I began thinking I had potential. My sister Rose Marie, had been the first basketball player in the family. Unfortunately, at the time, there were no athletic scholarships for women. Then came Mary. She was four years older and ended up going to Jones Junior College, then onto Nichols State. I went to a lot of her basketball games, both in high school and college. That's when I began to develop a much larger dream. I started to see how excelling at something like basketball could take you to so many new places. I began dreaming that this could happen to me.

The dream became clearer as I watched the colleges recruit Maeola. That fueled my interest. Now, basketball was much more than a sport that I played for entertainment or the passing of time on our farm. I practiced so much the rubber texture of the ball had stained my hands. My thirst for a good basketball game was unquenchable. I had arrived at the same point Maeola had departed from earlier. I never wanted to let go of this adrenaline-pumped game again; my relationship with basketball was now personal. In my junior year at McLain High, I really began to focus on my playing. When Maeola decided to go to Auburn University, my head turned. I was always excited to see her play and I became wrapped up in the idea that one day that this could be my world too. When I saw her, I also saw myself and the dream came closer to reality. It was also my first real glimpse of something beyond McLain, beyond the fields and trees. I was beginning to see that this world is bigger than I could have ever imagined.

Maeola was a star as a freshman undergraduate at Auburn University and I knew I'd have to work hard to be as good. My dream was to play alongside her on the Auburn University team. She became an All-American as a freshman and was runner up for the National Player of the Year Award. I saw her tremendous success and this empowered me to work harder to pursue my dream. My experience can serve as a valuable lesson to everyone. It begins with a premise that everyone should learn: nothing comes easy.

By the time I was a senior in high school, all I could focus on was my dream of following Maeola to Auburn University. But first things needed to come first. Maeola had been the best player on our high school team the year before, but we were still very good after she graduated. This only pushed us to work harder to reach the state championship game, a game we had also won the year before. So once again I had to focus on a short term dream—to win this game and be state champions once more. But it was one of those nights when we just couldn't get it going. With five minutes to play we were losing by 10 points. The dream was beginning to slip away.

At that point, I remember thinking that if we don't win at least we made it here. But our coach wouldn't let it go. He called a time out and told us flat out that if we gave up and lost, then we could no longer make excuses. We had to battle until the very last second. Suddenly, the dream was alive again and we all went out on the court, determined to turn it up a notch. The game began to go our way and with just 10 seconds left we were down by a single point and we had the ball.

All I could think of then was that I had to do this for my team. I got the ball and tried to look for a shot. With the clock ticking down I started to get set for a very long shot, a tough one to make. That's when I saw my niece and teammate (Tammy) under the basket. She was wide open and I whipped the ball to her for a layup. We had won! We had done it, despite losing our best player from the year before (Maeola) and had overcome all of the pressure. In a nutshell, we had spoiled the other team's party because we refused to surrender. We wouldn't give up our dream. I learned then, that even when you feel you're giving it your all, you can still push a little harder. We all have more inside us than we think. We must learn to reach inside for that extra strength.

Winning that game made me realize how beautiful it was to dream about something and then have it come true. There was a lot of hard work in between, nevertheless, the hardest to endure is often the sweetest to recall! To make something like that happen after it looks as if it won't happen is really like a dream. It was an exhilarating moment for all of us.

But winning the state championship was just the beginning. Now what followed was the pursuit of a much bigger dream: to follow Maeola to Auburn University. The rule was that a recruit could go on five-school visits. While I felt I wanted to go to Auburn University, I also looked forward to seeing other schools. What a dream! Then, imagine how I felt when, after winning the championship as a high school senior, I didn't receive any letters or phone calls from the schools I wanted. None showed any interest—including the University of Tennessee, Louisiana State University, the University of Mississippi, Mississippi State University, the University of Florida, and Auburn University. Talk about a dream being shattered! These were all schools that recruited my sister very heavily. In fact, there were at least 15 of them and, at the time, the recruiters said they eventually wanted both sisters. Looking back, they were probably saying that to try to entice Maeola and my parents.

Needless to say, this was extremely discouraging. I really thought some of them would be interested in me. Imagine how let down I felt when I heard things like *we missed the best sister so we don't want to waste our time with the other sister.* We had won the state championship two years in a row and now not a single school was showing interest in me. Even the University of Southern Mississippi, located in Hattiesburg just 30 minutes from our home, decided not to put any energy into recruiting me because their efforts to recruit Maeola had been in vain.

Like most people in my situation, part of me began to question whether all this was worth it, and whether this was a dream I should continue pursuing. I even thought about giving up basketball. My confidence began to fade. That's how easy it is to give up a dream. If you become discouraged, the situation suddenly looks hopeless. But that wasn't the end of it.

Persevering Against the Odds

Despite the rejection, I still wasn't ready to give up. The dream of following in my sister's footsteps was still strong. I decided to call Auburn University and basically ask, "What about me?" They told me they would get back to me, and when they did they invited me for a visit. Auburn University paid for the trip and I went there by myself on a Greyhound bus. I could feel the excitement all over again, thinking I would now be reunited with my sister. After an eight-hour bus ride, I finally arrived and was invited to the coach's house for dinner. What he said after dinner was even more of a shock than not having schools recruit me.

"I know you were set to come here and play," he said, "but there's no easy way to say this. You're not good enough to play here. You won't make the travel squad. Your sister will be discouraged and you'll be discouraged because you will not get much playing time. What we can do is help you get into another school."

Talk about having the air let out of you! I should have seen it coming. By making me take a bus, they were trying to show they weren't really interested. Whereas they had made the effort to fly my sister down for her visit. What they were doing for me was more of a courtesy. Perhaps they knew all along they didn't want me. I felt I was brought to Auburn University so they could tell me I couldn't play there, that I wasn't good enough. What could I say? I not only felt rejected, but I also felt ambushed. My heart became heavy with the feeling that life wasn't fair. How could they do this to me? Then, they had someone drive me back home. I might have needed a place of solitude, but it wasn't in the back seat of that car. This was one of the lowest moments of my life, seeing my ultimate dream all but evaporate before my eyes.

As soon as I reached home, my dad asked me what happened. I was upset and crying, and told him I should have known, that they said I wasn't good enough to play. Dad, as always, stayed calm and positive. He explained the things I should consider and the choices I had to make. He reminded me that *life is 10 percent what happens and 90 percent how you respond*. They had given me the option of coming to Auburn University, but I shouldn't expect to play until my third year. Dad asked me what I really wanted to do. I said I wanted to go to Auburn University and play alongside my sister. He could see I really wanted this for myself, to embrace the challenge, but needed the right attitude.

"You may have to work harder than others, but you'll be fine," my dad said, reassuringly. After we talked for another ten minutes, I felt as if a huge weight had been lifted off my shoulders. Dad believed so strongly in me and was so calm about it—I was rejuvenated. I knew if I went to Auburn University, I would have to develop an amazing work ethic. I would be the only player coming out for the team that they didn't really want. But when someone believes in you the way Dad did, it means everything. That faith allows you to keep your dream alive.

Ruthie Bolton, Auburn University Head Coach and Team, 1987

I was admitted to Auburn University in the fall of 1985. I had good enough grades, but I knew they did it out of loyalty to my sister, who had a great freshman year. Maybe they thought if they rejected me outright Maeola would want to leave. On top of that, they gave me a full scholarship. I wondered if that was because they probably didn't expect me to stay. They most certainly didn't think I would rise to the challenge. Though the coach said I might be able to play some by my junior year, I knew he was just being nice. But you can't make a dream come true by running away from it. In spite of all the challenges I faced, I knew I had to press on and show my resilience.

Now I had to put some of those principles I mentioned when dealing with dreams into practice. Here was a naysayer criticizing me, a coach telling me I wouldn't play because I wasn't good enough. I couldn't accept that. I had to stay positive. First, I asked myself if I really wanted this. The answer was a resounding YES! Then what did I have to do next? The answer was the old formula—to work hard and then work even harder. If they told me I wasn't quick enough, I'd think about what I'd have to do to be quicker. If they said I couldn't shoot well enough, I'd practice my shot and then practice it some more. "I will get better," I told myself.

Look at it this way: criticism is another person's perspective, but he or she doesn't always know everything about you. Rather, they just react to what they see or what they think they see at that moment. But you can't judge a book by its cover. You have to control what's on the inside of you. "It's what's inside that really counts." Think about what it takes for you to make that dream a reality. So you have to constantly replace the negative with a positive. Most importantly, you must keep working. Don't be so easy to surrender to what people say.

Another thing you should do is to *visualize* your dream. Whether it's sports or academics, you should have a vision of what you want to achieve. Visualize yourself in that basketball uniform or being a doctor—whatever your dream might be. As I said earlier, write them down as well. By both visualizing and writing, you can give dreams a real shape in your mind. Before playing a game, I would often visualize what I wanted the outcome to be and I'd see it all play out in my mind. Work without a vision is like flying a plane without a navigator.

How could my Auburn University dream stay alive? It was a matter of continual hard work, improving my shooting and defense. I was more driven to make my dream a reality and spent more time than ever developing my skills. Because they didn't see me as a viable member of the team, I felt there was no room for error. Not only did I want to exceed all their expectations of me, but I also wanted to develop a stronger work ethic. The fact that my dad believed in me strengthened my drive to succeed. Knowing you have someone you look up to can empower you to work harder and never give up your dream.

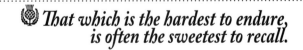

That which is the hardest to endure, is often the sweetest to recall.

The Dream Comes True

I worked my tail off the entire summer and continued to work hard during the fall when school began. By the time basketball practice started, I knew I was ready. I wanted to do more than what was asked of me, in other words, to go the extra mile. If the coach wanted us to do what we called a suicide sprint in 28 seconds, I wanted to do it in 25. I competed against myself. My work ethic enabled me to develop character and I saw how it was paying off. Every time I hit a roadblock I worked harder and overcame it. That builds confidence and gets you closer to the dream. It becomes second nature and a part of you. Soon, I knew no other way than to work hard and keep pushing.

Some people develop later than others. I was a late bloomer. The coach apparently wasn't sure how I would develop and didn't think I'd be effective that first year. But I was driven by my commitment to my dreams. I wanted to be the best at every drill, the strongest in the weight room, and the fastest up and down the court. I was extremely competitive, which helped motivate me. The negative comments also drove me to prove myself to everyone.

I knew Maeola had more raw talent and that I had to develop mine. I always felt it was inside of me and up to me to bring it out. I also had a lot of trust in Dad's opinion. He was the cornerstone of my life and an extremely positive person. Had he not believed in me so strongly, I may not have traveled as far down this road. You always need someone to believe in you and to encourage you. You may be able to do a lot on your own, but when you reach a crossroads, it helps to have someone there to give you an emotional boost and push. That's what my dad did for me and I am forever grateful. Thanks Dad!!!

Maeola

As I mentioned earlier, Maeola had a tremendous freshman year, becoming an All-American and runner-up for National Player of the Year. When I joined the team she was a sophomore and continued to play for four years. Our dreams had come true—we played together on the same college team for three years! She was a great big sister and role model. Maeola is a terrific cook and provided some wonderful college meals for us. Most importantly, she nurtured my spirit and taught me the importance of organization and planning. For fun, we sang together in the church after we were discovered by one of the workers at the university. Maeola played on one national team and went overseas to play for a couple of years in Italy and Spain. She was extremely talented. As hard as she worked, I felt she deserved a lot more than what she got. That's why I gave her my 1996 gold medal.

Mom, Dad and Maeola

As it turned out, I not only made the Auburn University team, but ended up starting halfway through my freshman season when another player was hurt. Our assistant coach, Carol Ross, told me that I should have been starting from the beginning.

**The Mississippi Girls,
Auburn University Team and Assistant Coach, 1987-88**

The coach, Joe Ciampi, finally told me that he had never seen a player transform so quickly. He never imagined I would step in and make an impact so soon. To me, it was a huge achievement since they had originally told me I'd be lucky to play by my junior year. The bottom line...
...I had made my biggest dream become a reality!

What I Learned
Making the team and then starting out my freshman year, proved to be a turning point in my life. It began to define me. It also taught me once

and for all, about what it takes for dreams to come true and I've used the same formula ever since. When the coach told me I'd be lucky to play by my junior year I could have easily chosen not to play basketball anymore, believing that I wasn't good enough. I knew I had some talent. Then I learned that if your talent is only a 4 or a 5, but your work ethic is an 8, 9, or 10—you can achieve just as much if not more than someone filled with raw talent. Sometimes, a player's talent may blossom late, but if you work really hard, your talent will eventually catch up. Going above and beyond made the difference.

❦ *It's what's inside that really counts.*

I could have also taken the easy way and gone to a smaller college. The University of Southern Mississippi would have taken me and told me that I could probably play right away. Instead I took the tougher road. I wanted to prove I was good enough for Auburn University. Making my dream a reality became a challenge and a very empowering experience. It showed me that all the things you go through, all the roadblocks, detours and tough breaks can be overcome and lead you to a beautiful place.

It all starts with the right mindset. If you don't have the drive and a positive mindset you are likely to make excuses and not make that dream happen. My career at Auburn University was extremely satisfying. We made two Final Fours in four years and it turned out to be just the beginning of a long basketball career that would take me to the Olympics, to different places around the world, and then to the WNBA. How did this happen? I had refused to give up my dream; I had refused to surrender. There is no substitute for hard work.

CHAPTER FOUR
DEVELOPING PASSION

Not only is developing passion one of my favorite topics, but I've found being passionate is one of the most important elements for a happy and successful life. Your passion enables you to pursue dreams and rise to challenges. My passion helped me overcome setbacks and ultimately achieve goals that at first seemed unreachable. You could almost say that passion is the engine that drives you and helps you reach whatever your chosen destination may be.

Passion keeps you alive and thriving. It's something you go to bed thinking about and wake up thinking about. Passion is deep, exciting and a force of its own. It keeps you focused and drives your purpose, giving you that extra zest for life, which ultimately fuels you and keeps you vibrant. The thing that drives my passion is the desire to be the best. When I played basketball, each game was new, exciting and different. Now when I speak in front of a group of kids, my passion for helping them fuels me, keeps me from being tired, and propels me to do more to help them realize they can also be the best in any area, no matter what happened to them.

Passion can affect every area of your life. There will be many things you like and enjoy, but you only become very passionate about a few things. I tell kids there will be many things that catch your eye, but only a few that touch your heart. Those touching your heart give you passion—pursue them. There have been times when I've enjoyed something, but became passionate about it when I began seeing the results. Working out is one example. Even with just three hours sleep, working out makes me feel better. It energizes me. I absolutely have to include it in my everyday lifestyle. My passion for basketball lasted for years. I still love it, and play every chance that I get. However, since I no longer play on a competitive level, I've transferred some of my passion for basketball to working with kids.

Trying to reach a goal or make a dream come true without passion will only make you do just what you feel you need to do, but no more. With passion, you'll go above and beyond the ordinary. If someone asks you to do 25 pushups a day, you do 30. When I'm scheduled to talk to a group for an hour, I might just stay for two hours. That's because my passion for every kid compels me to. My dad called it the "Can't Help It Syndrome." Passion overtakes you and drives you to do more.

Basketball Camp RuRu, 2005

Obviously, you can't be passionate about everything. You may, for instance, enjoy a TV show. I always loved *Leave It to Beaver*, *Sanford & Son*, and *Good Times*, to name a few. They relaxed me and reminded me of family and home. But if I missed a few weeks or some episodes that was okay—that kind of enjoyment isn't the same as passion.

I encourage kids to play a number of different sports, and to keep their grades up. Playing a variety of sports is good for personal development and physical fitness. As children grow older, they usually gravitate to the sport that gets them the most excited, and that's the one they'll develop a passion for. When you do a lot of different things, sooner or later you'll know what brings out your passion. It's almost as if the passion chooses you. I played volleyball and ran track, but basketball was the sport that fueled my passion. It gave me a feeling of fulfillment and led me to become the best I could be.

A Word to the Wise

One word of caution at this point: if pushed too hard by others and you do too much, too early, you can lose your passion. Some parents force kids to play, play, play—sports, music lessons, dance classes, etc. That kind of non-stop schedule can lead to burnout. Passion is great when you commit to it, but you can still get burned out. You need to find a balance. Passion becomes endangered when you don't allow breaks in your schedule. If you feel passionate about everything, you may also get burned out. You must pick and choose where your passions lie, or let them pick you. But make sure that balance is there, so you can keep the drive alive—the passion—for things you really love the most. Remember passions, like your body, must be nurtured. Keep your passions healthy.

Some Other Aspects of Passion

There are so many ways in which having passion can affect your entire life. It is impossible to list them. Being a passionate person will not only allow you to achieve so much more, but it will also help you through the down times and enable you to rebound faster after setbacks. Once you develop passion, it isn't automatic that you will always have it. Circumstances can sometimes make it difficult to keep going, especially when you have setbacks or fail to reach your goal despite your passion for it. You will sometimes have to fight within yourself to retain your passion. As I often say, "If a door closes, a window usually opens." In other words, you will find something else to be passionate about.

Keeping passion alive is extremely important since much of your future counts on it. People who lose their passion usually find they are not getting the results they hoped for. The thing to keep in mind is that you have to feel good about pushing yourself hard, even if you fall short of your goal. If you have the passion to pursue one thing, you can use that same passion to pursue another. Give yourself enough time to grow and mature before reaching too high for your age or skill level. When you don't give up, your passion will pay off one way or another. Passion made me take the unwanted bus ride that changed my life. You have to work with your passion to achieve your dreams!

Sometimes I'll meet 15 or 20 girls and all of them want to play in the WNBA. I encourage them to keep going and push for it, to follow their passion. The work you put in, the drive and enthusiasm you show for the game won't be in vain. If you don't get the results you want, the passion and work ethic that go with it will carry over to another area of your life. If you don't become the basketball player or the tennis player you want to be, your desire may eventually lead you to become a top coach, accountant, a doctor, a teacher, or a very important person in some other area you love. When you apply your passion to an area you love, it will lead you to conquer your competition.

I have a good friend, Mark Cruise, whose dream it was to play in the National Football League. He had talent and passion, and worked very hard. Yet he fell short after several chances with teams. His last tryout was with the Dallas Cowboys when Tom Landry was still the head coach. The day they were making player cuts, the famed UCLA basketball coach, John Wooden, was in town visiting Landry. When my friend Mark came out of the office, Coach Wooden could tell he had been released. Always a positive person who loved giving positive advice, Coach Wooden told him: "Don't worry son, all the hard work you spent trying to make the NFL will pay off for you somewhere else."

Twenty years later, my friend Mark saw Coach Wooden again at a book signing. He reminded the coach about what he had told him years earlier and how his kind words helped him. He had transferred his passion to finance and was now a successful accountant. He learned Coach Wooden's lesson and did not let discouragement choke his passion. He applied it to another area of his life. The key is not giving up, just moving on in another area of strength. That's exactly what my friend Mark did.

Ganon Baker, Basketball Trainer

Ganon Baker is a perfect example of how to use passion to pursue a dream in a slightly different way than originally envisioned. Ganon was an outstanding basketball player, a small point guard who was quick and very talented. He had a great shot. He tried out for the NBA but was slowed by an injury. When he came back he was hurt again. He absolutely loved basketball. When he fell short of fulfilling his dream, he vowed to help others reach theirs. He became an unbelievably great basketball teacher who conducts workshops all over the country. Because he couldn't get basketball out of his blood, he transferred his passion from playing to teaching, and probably became a greater teacher than he was as a player. His work ethic is amazing. He's leaves no room for error and says that every time he gets out on the court to teach, he imagines himself playing. He puts everything into it because he approaches each session as if it is the last time he'll ever teach. Now that's real passion!

🏵 *With passion, you'll go above and beyond the ordinary.*

Passion can also lead to another quality that can help you as you grow and mature—accountability. Everyone should be accountable for their actions. Passion gives you commitment and a sense of responsibility which keeps you accountable. Passion is a gift and you should be accountable to it, so much so that it will bother your conscience if you're slacking off and not giving 100 percent. I'm passionate about health and nutrition, for instance, but there are times when I'll find myself eating too many sweets. I reluctantly stop eating sweets and check myself. The accountability to my passion always reminds me of the requirements to be in top physical shape to be competitive in basketball.

It's the accountability to your passion that drives you to do your best and be your best. Passion will eventually become part of your DNA. Properly nurtured, it becomes second nature. I'm trying to learn to play golf and want to enjoy it while I try to master it. While I may not be as passionate about golf as I was about basketball, I know I'm passionate about my work ethic and will always try to do the best I can. It's the same work ethic I had while growing up and cleaning the yard or picking cucumbers. I always wanted to be better than I was the day before. So, always live in the moment and let your passion serve you and stay accountable.

Young people and adults have at least one or more passions which may lead to success. The more things you pursue, the less likely you'll go out and do crazy things. Passion leads to the productive use of your time as you naturally listen to your inner winner. Passion gives you a sense of purpose, structure and direction. Every young person wants to feel that he or she belongs. If you don't have passion you can end up "belonging" to a passionless group that has no focus, ambition, or a good track record of accomplishments. Passion drives you to belong to the right group at the right time. Remember, if you don't stand for something, you'll fall for anything.

I know how important it is for young people to be occupied with positive things. My passion now is to help kids find their passion. It excites them and helps them feel good about themselves. According to a study done by Nike, girls who have a passion for sports are less likely to be overweight, get pregnant, drop out of school or do drugs. Many girls who become pregnant at a young age find it extremely difficult to achieve their dreams. But, when they begin to express themselves through sports, music and other hobbies they discover passions that lead them to positive groups and activities that help them achieve the dreams they envisioned.

Ruthie with Larasha Ludd

Passion plus talent will keep a person accountable. Accountability encourages you to get ready for the next game, or to sing or dance at the next talent show. Passion overcomes challenges and keeps dreams alive. It gives you a sense that "I'm somebody and I'm doing something that is worthwhile." Passion helps you discover who you really are.

It took a lot of life lessons to teach me the importance of passion. It's an attitude and a mindset. It was instilled in my family over and over by my dad. A positive attitude was extremely important to him. He felt it was the foundation of a successful life-path. When he told you to take the trash out, he didn't want to see your body language change or hear you give out a sigh of resentment. He wouldn't put up with it. He gave you a command and you said, *"Yes, sir!"* He was teaching structure and the effectiveness of a positive attitude. He also taught us how accountability and how a positive attitude were related. I learned then that nothing is ever accomplished with excellence without enthusiasm and a positive mental attitude. An important question I could ask myself daily was: "How do I positively embrace the day's activities or the next challenge?"

Once you begin to embrace life with a positive attitude and enthusiasm, it makes your days more fun. Before long you'll find that a positive attitude and enthusiasm become a mindset. At first, you become passionate for a moment. With continuous practice, you'll find you are passionate for longer periods of time. It radiates from you, almost like an aura, and this aura attracts even more success into your life. Life is full of many small, passionate moments and that's what eventually builds into something great. It's all part of the process of becoming who you are, believing in and enjoying those small moments of passion.

Passion also helps you work through adversity. To do that, your passion must become your comfort zone, a safe place where you are in charge and in control. You've got to allow passion to take you to a place of confidence, a peaceful paradise where you enjoy your gift and share it with others. Remember, there will be adversity in your life. It's a normal part of growing up to feel lost from time to time. Life is a journey, use your passions to get back on track.

When you do have some adversity, create a "passion back-up plan." For example, when I'm dealing with some unpleasant issues, I'll go out and run or maybe go to the gym and work out. Working out is such a passion with me that doing it almost feels like a mini-vacation. It not only keeps me in shape, it puts me into a place of solitude and always makes me feel that things will be all right. Even as a kid, when I was going through some tough times, I thought of something I was excited about to wake up for the next morning. It was my jump start to get back on track. Try this out; it works!

Another thing you can do during some difficult moments is to write about your passion. That's another way to bring yourself back. I often ask young girls who have a passion for basketball to write down the reasons why they want to excel in the sport. In doing this they discover things about themselves and their passion that they find exciting. Writing is not only a release, it can help you address the adversity you're dealing with. It allows you to put things in perspective. No one can operate at 100 percent all the time. Passion is a beautiful thing that heals your soul and guides you to positive actions that make life worthwhile.

It wasn't easy for me to excel at basketball. I thought I was good in high school, but I was not recruited by a college. I had to call on my passion and work even harder than I had even done before. My rewards were making the Auburn University basketball team and then becoming a starter by mid-season of my freshman year. This was just the beginning of a long and successful basketball career. I never lost my passion for the sport. But, being a good college athlete isn't the only important thing. You also have to get good grades to continue playing and remain in school.

I wasn't always the best student. Getting the kind of grades I needed was sometimes difficult. I took advantage of tutors they offered at Auburn University and worked very hard. My work ethic and passion is what helped me with what could have been a very tough academic situation. Because I knew I had overcome adversities in basketball, I felt I could also do the same in school. It was my passion that helped me tackle academics and ultimately succeed. In fact, I made the All-Academic team twice!

It's what you learn from having passion for one thing that can be applied to other areas of your life, even if you have to push yourself to get there. I came across this kind of situation when I began speaking to groups of kids. I was relentless in other areas, but when I first began speaking I found it frightening. My passion to help children was so great, I knew I just had to push myself to overcome this fear. The adversity I had to go through in basketball gave me the strength to take on and ultimately conquer my fear of speaking in public. Passion helps conquer your fears. It allows you to go beyond the ordinary and never settle. It makes your entire life better.

Steps to Developing Passion

Having passion simply helps you to go through life easier. Many people discover their passion without help or advice. Some also find passion and, for a variety of reasons, lose it. Here then, are some basic rules for developing and ultimately keeping your passion:

1. Find that one thing you can't do without. Look at life as a buffet of choices. Then decide which one or two things lead you to develop the "biggest appetite." You may have several for a period a time, but at some point you'll discover the one thing you feel you can't do without. You have now found your passion.

2. Let time tell. The more you begin to enjoy something, the more you'll find yourself in the environment that goes with it. Whether it's a sport or something else, such as music, you'll gradually find yourself doing that more and more. You'll devote more time to it consistently. That's how passion develops.

3. Develop your skills. At the beginning you may not be very good at the thing you're beginning to love the most. Say, it's playing the piano. Though you still aren't that good, you already enjoy it and dream about playing the piano in front of many people. The passion and dreams you have for it will lead you to taking lessons and practicing more. You'll see your improvement and you'll continue to move forward. Practice fuels your passion. In fact, Malcolm Gladwell, a famous author of *Outlier* and *Blink*, shows how 10,000 hours of practice in most any area leads to expertise and mastery.

4. Strike a balance. Even though you're developing a passion for something, don't neglect other parts of your life. Don't let your passion consume you to the point where only one thing is important. Then it becomes an obsession. Learn what else is important in your life. My dad was passionate about the need for church and a spiritual life and we knew we had to share that with him. My passion to play basketball was always stronger than the desire to sit in church. But, I knew that I needed to share my dad's passion to be able to play basketball outside later. This balance allowed me to pursue my passion.

5. Don't allow your passion to become an obsession. This is very important. Learn to be smart about your passion. If you are passionate about surfing, for example, you need to know not to go out in dangerous waters. Once you forget about boundaries and safety, you are on your way to becoming obsessed. If you have an injury and can't perform, that's another boundary you shouldn't cross. If you have a passion for running but become ill and are told by a doctor to take five days off, do it. If you continue because you feel you *have* to, you may end up hurting yourself and derailing your future. Always stay on the positive side of safety. Your future depends on it.

6. Learn the correct way to pursue your passion. Once you discover your passion always ask questions. What skills do I need? Who can help me improve? How do I practice to improve? Try to find someone in the field who can tell you what to expect and how to thrive and nurture yourself. That

will make it real. Read stories about how others got started, how they overcame their challenges and what it took for them to reach the top.

7. Don't do too much too soon. Once you develop passion for something you want to move quickly. But don't expect to become an expert overnight. There will be setbacks. Be prepared not to give up quickly. The way I always looked at it was that *a setback is a setup for a comeback*. Remember, some people get faster results than others. You should look at your life goal more like a marathon than a sprint. For most, it takes time. Just let your passion take you there one step at a time. Set goals to improve every day and learn from your mistakes. There will be times when you plateau, reaching a sticking point. Once you know that happens, you can work through it and find the activities and actions to break through the plateau.

8. Have passion for more than one thing. If you find you've developed passion for two or more things, don't feel that you immediately have to pick one. I have a nephew, Johnas Street, who has a passion for both basketball and music. He even made it through the first rounds of the American Idol television show competition before being eliminated. He continues to pursue his passion for singing and basketball and keeps everything in balance. If you have a burning desire to pursue two things, go right ahead, just remember to keep the rest of your life in balance. Maybe the window of opportunity will close for one and you can then pursue the other. Things will work out in the end. And, as always, passion will take you there.

9. Beware of burnout. This is something for all young people to watch out for. I've spent time with kids who have developed a passion and a drive, then suddenly slack off. Some children, may play ball all year round and forget to make time to just be kids. Take time to do everyday things and share your life with family and friends. Overindulging in your passion can be detrimental. Signs of burnout include fatigue, depression, closing yourself off from other people, loss of enthusiasm and, finally, self-doubt. You can push so hard that you hit a wall. When you see these signs or others see them in you, it's time to slow down and regroup. Take a deep breath, and regain your balance. Your passion will return if it is the right thing for you.

Balancing her life with family, 2007 (Ruthie, nieces and god-child)

The All-Important Balance

One of my good friends has a son who loves basketball. He was passionate about it and worked very hard to improve his game. He said everything was going great; told his mom all was fine. Then, when his report card came, he had failed every class except physical education. He lost focus on all his academic subjects. It could be he was so focused on basketball, totally in the zone, that he neglected his schoolwork. Grades are what usually suffer first when kids become unbalanced. They prefer to pursue just their passion rather than concentrate on school. Passion is certainly a great thing, but the fundamentals cannot be ignored. This not only includes schoolwork, but everything from brushing your teeth and getting enough rest to eating well. Finally, never lock out your friends and family because of your passion. They are likely the ones who will tell you that you're off track and give you positive energy and support when you need it!

The important thing is to develop your passion as you grow and mature. Passion can only help you achieve your dreams in life. Never be afraid of it or talked out of it. All the above steps explain the right way to find and nurture your passion. They also alert you to some of the pitfalls. If a passion for something hasn't overtaken you yet, don't fret. If you understand what passion is all about, there's a good chance you'll discover it in the years ahead. When something strikes you as special and worth pursuing, go for it. Then, you'll find your passion for sure.

The Rewards of Having Passion

Passion is really a win-win situation. For openers, it gives you a great deal of self-satisfaction. You'll realize you can achieve things with passion you might not have thought possible. Passion builds confidence and helps you improve your work ethic. It spills over to other areas of your life. Even if you fall short of achieving a goal or a certain level of success, people will watch and admire you for the way you work and give it your all. You will not only learn from your efforts, but your passionate experiences will motivate others.

Passion is a special kind of energy that draws people to you and gives you the ability to change another person's life. This energy will radiate out to others from you. In some ways, it can be contagious. The person who has developed passion goes further and achieves more. The person who has natural ability and intelligence, but lacks passion, always seems to fall short in one way or another. Without passion, you won't find many of the rewarding things life has to offer. To me, it's a crime to see talent and intelligence go to waste.

There was a girl at Auburn University who was on the basketball team with me. She was tall, talented, and had received a basketball scholarship. Vickie had a lot of natural ability, so much so that she could have a bad game and still finish with good numbers. She could go through the motions and still have 20 points and 12 rebounds. One year, she was a three time Kodak All-American. There was just one thing missing: passion. I remember times when she wanted to quit. Her passion was to get married and have children. If she had that same passion for basketball, she could have been a WNBA Star. But she always wanted to work with kids and that's what she ended up doing. She followed her passion and that's great. Everyone has a right to find his or her own passion. Basketball didn't give her the reward she wanted, but working with kids did.

If you have passion, you can always see the reward that is waiting for you. If you don't, you may be pretty good at something but you won't see the possibilities or the rewards. There are times when you can force yourself to be passionate because you know what the rewards will be. I see kids who are passionate about school, focused and studying all the time. Some of them may be forcing the passion because they know the benefits and rewards of good grades and a good education. Maybe their real passion is the thing they are striving for once their education is finished. They won't make it without the grades, so they transfer their passion to their studies as a stepping stone to achieve the great career they desire and will most likely obtain.

People who have passion stand out. You can see it in their body language especially in their eyes. It's said that *the eyes are the window to the soul*. People with passion smile; they radiate confidence. There's a teacher at Jackman Middle School, just where I speak who radiates passionate energy. When I asked about him, I was told he had been at the school for more than ten years and still works with kids 13 or 14 hours a day. He never seemed to get tired and was always smiling in great spirits. He is the Director of Health and Human Affairs and he does great things for the students and their parents. It's apparent that this man gets tremendous gratification from what he does. As a result, he makes a huge impact on the kids. He's not just earning a paycheck; he's following his passion and experiencing the rewards. What a wonderful life!

Passion as a Way of Life

As far as I'm concerned, passion should be a required way of life. Without it, life is boring. There's no way around that. If you don't find passion, you'll only exist; you won't thrive. There will be no real substance to your life, no purpose or drive. Passion adds joy and excitement. It fuels your smile. It's a building block to your successful life-path. It gives you an action agenda, a destination, and helps your dreams take shape.

When I became passionate about basketball and was accepted into Auburn University, a basketball career became my target. I realized, I should actually go to the next level in this game. I told myself, "It would be great to play on the national team." So I started focusing on getting to the next level and making it my passion. Passionate people give 110 percent. When I speak to young boys and girls, I want them to see the passion in me. When I give my heart, they give me their hands and ears and listen to my message—they connect to what I'm saying and understand.

Passion also increases creativity. When a passionate person hits a roadblock, he or she avoids excuses and finds a way around it. They don't take no for an answer. Passion makes you think more deeply to broaden your horizons and enhance your potential. If you are passionate, you'll seek out more knowledge and learn more about how to succeed in life. You'll read more, which will broaden your vocabulary. Passion leads to greater success.

A Rewarding Encounter

When I was playing for the Sacramento Monarchs, I would see a man at Arco Arena all the time. We would talk for 30 seconds. I didn't even know his name at first, but I liked the vibrant energy in him and knew he was a positive person. The last year I played in the WNBA, I saw him at one of the games and he said he wanted to share something with me. His name was Mr. Peterson. He told me that several months earlier, he had suffered an brain aneurysm, passed out at Arco Arena, and was in a coma for three weeks. He could hear people talking but couldn't respond. The only people seeing him were family and close friends. But he said that two other people came into his mind—me and Chris Webber, who also played for the Sacramento Kings. We were his two favorite players. He said he heard my voice telling him to hold on. Then he said, "You helped save my life." That gave me chills. I was thankful to God that Chris and I were his angels. We were obviously kindred spirits, and that's how passionate people connect.

I saw something special in Mr. Peterson: friendliness and positive energy. Mr. Peterson worked in customer service, embraced people, and exemplified passion. They held his job until he recovered and returned to work. His parting words to me were, "You will always have a special place in my heart. You gave me hope." I can't tell you how good that made me feel!

Ruthie Bolton with Mr. Peterson in 2005

The Qualities of Passion

By now, I'm sure you realize just how much having passion means to me. It is always one of the cornerstones of my talks with kids and something I urge young people to seek because it will fuel the rest of their lives. I'm going to list the major qualities you usually find in a person with passion. They are positive qualities everyone should strive for. If you find yourself with these qualities, you have undoubtedly also found the key to the wonderful world of passion.

In no special order, passionate people are:

1. Energetic
2. Joyful
3. Ambitious and goal oriented
4. Focused
5. Driven
6. Confident

7. Inquisitive
8. People who make things happen
9. Personable with social skills
10. Easy to be around
11. Uncomplaining
12. Blessed with a desire to learn
13. Seek and take advice
14. People of action
15. Less Fearful
16. Most apt to look you straight in the eye

Think of me looking you straight in the eye right now. Then listen. Work to develop your passion. You'll never regret it.

CHAPTER FIVE
SETTING AND REACHING GOALS

In the last two chapters, I discussed the importance of beginning to dream and then developing passion. In this chapter, you'll begin to see how everything is related through goal setting. Dreaming is the first step to setting goals. Passion helps you reach your goals. It's all part of taking the best actions to enjoy a productive and positive life. That is something I believe everyone can achieve, if they keep moving forward and working hard.

Setting goals gives a person direction, a sense of focus and an agenda. When you set small goals when you're young, it marks the beginning of a journey that will take you to a definite place, hopefully a place of your choosing. When you set goals, you set standards and expectations for yourself. Goal setting helps you measure your accountability to yourself. The achievement of a goal, gives you something to look forward to. When you wake up in the morning and there is a specific goal to be achieved, it gives you structure and direction. It can strengthen your focus, and stop you from wasting valuable time on things that are not related to your goal.

It's a positive thing to set goals, and then try your best to reach them. Without having goals — a thing to aim for, you can easily find yourself lost or unable to make the needed adjustment to achieve your goal. People without goals tend to be sad, treading water without a real grasp on their lives. They lack purpose and that leads to sadness. Without goals, your life lacks luster. You exist but may not have the feeling of being really alive. Sometimes, you may be unable to express yourself or put your finger on what may be causing you to feel unhappy, unproductive, or unfulfilled. Make yourself feel better by setting and achieving goals.

When To Start Setting Goals

I think most children subconsciously begin setting goals at the age of five or six without even realizing it. They just begin to think, *this is what I want to do and accomplish.* By the third grade, most understand what goals are. If you know what you want to do by then it's an amazing thing.

Even if you change your mind later it's still beautiful to have goals and ambition. It starts you moving toward one thing. If that doesn't work, you move toward the next. Soon after realizing what goals are, children begin to understand the difference between short and long term goals. A short term goal can be accomplished within a year; a long term goal may take several years to accomplish.

When you are young it's okay to have a long term goal; what you think you want to be someday. But it's the short term goals that are immediately reachable—being a good student, doing your homework, making it to the next grade, being a good son or daughter and a good brother or sister. In fact, the younger the child, the smaller the goals should be so they are reachable. That way, the child remains encouraged. Both parents and teachers should encourage children to set and achieve goals. Kids have so much energy, that having goals gives them direction and structure. Goal setting and goal accomplishments help children to discover what they are really passionate about.

When young children begin playing sports, give them small goals whether they are really good or just average performers. Set achievable goals and encourage them to accomplish them. Meet them where they are. Short term goals encourage youth to get better at their individual skills. For example, one child may make eight of ten free throws but another struggles and makes just three or four out of ten. Have the less proficient shooter set a goal of making five of ten free throws by the following week and tell him not to be concerned about what the others do. Share the smile on his or her face when the goal is reached!

The Need for Reinforcement

I remember working with 13 and 14 year old girls, coaching them on how to set screens. It's a matter of timing and positioning, and you have to work hard to get it right. One girl just had no clue. I told her to put her foot in a certain spot and make sure her body was right there. I broke it down in plain language and she begins improving rapidly. Then, I made it a point to tell her how she improved so much in a short time. She was behind everyone, but felt some sense of accomplishment because she finally began getting it. Besides setting a goal, you have to reinforce it and let kids know it's okay if they can't do something well immediately. They have to keep working. Children need a lot of reinforcement, especially when they see their peers reaching goals with no problem and they aren't. Short term goals have to be reachable so kids don't become discouraged. That's important.

Short and Long Term Goals

It's a good thing to have a major long term goal with many short term goals in between. These act as steps toward achievement of the bigger goal. But, be careful. Long term goals can be overwhelming when you're very young. That's why it's important to have the small goals first. They will keep you occupied and focused on the task just ahead. As long as you're motivated and keep moving forward, the long term goal will become clearer and within reach. If the long term goal is to go to college and play a major sport, then the short term goals can be things like joining a gym and working to get stronger and quicker, and to develop the individual skills you'll need to succeed. You must also go to class, keep your grades up and track your workouts. So when you are young, you must dedicate yourself to the perfection of your short term goals.

Short term goals don't necessarily have to be related to long term goals. I often ask kids about their goal in life. I hear things like I want to be a doctor, teacher, athlete, and beautician. No matter what your goals are, you need a solid character, a positive attitude and a strong work ethic. That's what I teach. Become a better person and you'll also be able to achieve more in the long term. And remember, if you have a long term goal, continue to set short term goals all along the way. When you achieve them, they uplift and encourage you.

Another thing to remember is to always reassess your goals, especially if things don't seem to be working out the way you planned. Maybe you didn't prioritize correctly or, you may be doing something wrong in pursuit of your goals. At this point, you usually need direction from someone. Don't ever hesitate to ask for advice or someone's input. It's your journey, but you may be going in the wrong direction. Find a person who is knowledgeable about the goal you're pursuing—someone who can give you the right advice, whether it's changing a practice technique, working harder or finding a way to alter your routine.

If it's a short term goal and you're not making progress you have to find a way to overcome it. Learn what works and what doesn't. You will often need help to do that, so don't become discouraged. One of my short term goals as a kid was to jump over an old fence. My sister did it like a high jumper because she had long legs. Her body was different from mine and I couldn't do it that way. So I had to try it a different way. I had to find what worked for me. I experimented with different styles and found one that worked. That's how I reached my goal. Have people challenge you and ask for help. It shows that you want to learn and get better, that you want to do things the right way. It shows your good work ethic.

There is something else everyone should watch for when they begin setting goals: only set goals that are attainable, whether short or long term. It may be nice to have a goal to be President of the United States, but a very select few will get there. Be realistic. When you set a realistic goal, people around you see your progress. When you achieve it, you feel better about yourself and build momentum. You get more results because you're excited about your progress. How, then, can you be sure your goal is realistic and attainable?

Once again, you need input from other people; people who can honestly help you evaluate your goals and your chances of reaching them. Sometimes you need another set of eyes, especially from someone you trust. You can even ask directly if they think your goal is attainable. They might say yes, it is. However, they will explain what you have to do and provide guidance about the steps you can take to improve. Then, you have to ask yourself if you have the ability and willingness to do all it will take. You'll have to make some sacrifices, but you'll also have to keep the important things in your life in balance.

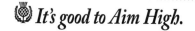 *It's good to Aim High.*

Unrealistic goals are those that are simply set too high for one reason or another. Some people want to challenge themselves. It is good to aim high. While sometimes a noble idea, it can also lead to disappointment and discouragement. When you don't see progress, you may lose your excitement or have more failures than successes. You can easily burn out. When that happens, the joy from pursuing your goals will disappear. Your commitment may wane. You may lower the time you put into it. That's when you have to step away and reassess the situation. You might even want to get some good advice about your goals, find out why you aren't reaching them, or why you tend to set them too high. Pump yourself up by setting reachable goals.

Remember, some goals may not be realistic early on, but five years later you'll be ready to reach for them. If I had said I wanted to be a college basketball star, play in the Olympics and then go on to a professional basketball career when I was 10 years old, while living in a small Mississippi town that would have certainly been viewed as an unrealistic goal. I just didn't have the skills then to wake up as a world class basketball player. Fortunately, I tended to set short term goals then. It took a long time for me to develop the skills and determination to achieve the longer goals. As I watched my sister Maeola achieve basketball success, it encouraged me to keep trying. By the time I entered college, my goal was well within reach and I went after it with everything I had.

Life Can Change Your Goals

Now that I have a daughter and son, my goals have changed. Now my agenda has to include them. Their needs come first. I can still set goals, but I have to make some sacrifices for my children. Last year, I wanted to attend an event in Italy but had no one to take care of my daughter Hope and my son Christofer, so I couldn't go. My biggest goal now is always to be a mother first. That doesn't mean I still can't have other goals, short and long term. It's just that my children have changed the structure of my life. And that's why I tell people to keep a balance and stay focused on the most important things in your life.

Ruthie with her 1-year old daughter Hope, in 2010

Tips for Setting and Reaching Goals

It doesn't take a rocket scientist to understand the concept of setting and reaching goals. It's a relatively simple premise. You find something you want to do and want to do well, and you begin to pursue it. Excelling at your chosen endeavor becomes your goal. But, as we've already discussed, reaching a goal isn't always easy. Short term goals keep you focused; they also keep you moving forward toward that long term goal. A short term goal gives you a chance to grow, mature, and determine whether your long term goal is what you really want. Then you can refocus on a long term goal that's best for you. Here, then, are some additional tips that will help you reach all of your goals while keeping a positive attitude and avoiding discouragement.

1. Seek help. Seeking help is an important tool for anyone working to reach their goals. It's very difficult to do it alone. Go to people with whom you are comfortable, those you feel you can trust. It can be your parents, a coach, a teacher, a good friend, an older brother or sister, or a clergyman. You should also look for someone who has experience in your field of endeavor. He or she can give you valuable insight.

A parent once came to me because her daughter's goal was to reach the next level as a basketball player. She wanted to know just what it would take for her daughter to achieve her goal, so I went to watch her play. I saw immediately that she had to get stronger and work on her ball handling. I not only gave her some suggestions and drills on how to do this, but also told her what to watch out for, things that might hurt her, such as training too much and losing her balance with grades, family obligations and friends.

Nobody can reach their goals alone. When you're very young you can reach those first, small goals through trial and error. As you become older and have more ambitious goals, that is when you are more likely to need direction and should reach out to someone more experienced in your specialty. When you hit a sticking point and stop making progress, that's another time to seek help. You can be motivated and passionate yet still going about it the wrong way. Working toward your goals the right way is extremely important. There are always resources out there—people, books, and the internet. Find people with experience who support your goals. It's a great investment in your own progress.

2. Persevere. The more realistic short term goals you reach, the more successful you'll be. If you don't quite reach a goal, however, you still need that desire to go on and fight. Find another way to reach it. You have to develop the stamina to persevere. If a goal gets into your heart and soul, you'll find a way to keep going. While long term goals can be overwhelming at times, the ability to reach short term goals will build your confidence for the long run. One trick to persevere with a long term goal is to make it part of a series of short term goals. Tackle it in steps. Reach the first step and you'll have the confidence to reach the next, and so on. It also makes it seem that the long term goal is on the back burner when you concentrate on a series of short term steps. If you don't have enough of these interim goals, the long term goal can overwhelm and fatigue you.

3. Always Visualize. When I joined the Olympic team, one of the first things the coach did was show us several minutes of videos, first of teams that lost games in the last minute, then teams that won in the last minute.

Ruthie and the USA Olympic Team posing for Sports Illustrated in 1998, after the team won the World Championship

He then said, "Imagine which you want to experience, winning or losing. Visualize yourself standing there on the podium and having a gold medal put around your neck." That's what I did, visualized myself standing in victory in Atlanta at the 1996 Olympics. But then I put it on the back burner because I knew there would be a lot of work to do before we got there. Both my teammates and I started with small goals first and any time we began feeling discouraged, we again visualized standing on that podium. Then we would begin working and pushing each other again. That's how we eventually won it!

Visualization helps. It can help you with anything—from getting an A on a test to singing well in the church choir, finishing first in a race or winning an Olympic Gold Medal. It helps build confidence and helps you to relax into the win. When you are tense, you block your own power, so you definitely want to visualize from a positive standpoint. It will clear your mind, relax you and give you the best chance to achieve your goals. Even if achieving that long term goal is still years away, visualizing it paints a picture, makes it real, puts it within reach and gives you a feeling that it is attainable. It's almost like daydreaming, but it really works and always puts you in a good place.

4. Stick with it. Children need help to continue pursuing their goals. It can be up to friends, parents, teachers, and coaches—anyone who has that person's best interests at heart. How then, do you help someone stick with it, especially if they have come up short several times and feel discouraged? It's important that children, from an early age, see the purpose of setting goals. All children want something; few know how to begin to get it. Children from challenging homes often get mixed signals. Some of them are angry. Very few of them write their goals down. As a result, they fail to hold onto the picture that keeps them accountable to their goals and they lose hope for the future.

When children aren't serious or don't commit to what it takes to reach their short term goals, other dedicated friends or family members may help them find out what they really want to do. They can help a child discover why they aren't pursuing their passion, or why they are giving up too easily. Why isn't goal setting working? Perhaps the child just needs constant reinforcement. Some children from challenging homes have a low attention span, or a bad self-image, which they often get from home or from their peers. That's why reinforcement from somewhere is so important. With support, they will gain more confidence and get into the routine of working toward something and sticking to it. If they are not getting that support and reinforcement at home, they need to seek constant help from someone else they trust.

If you aren't reaching your goals as quickly as others, it's important you don't compare yourself to them. You only have to answer to yourself.

It's okay if you aren't progressing as quickly as your friends. The important thing is that you keep making progress, keep working toward that goal. People you trust should encourage you and that's why you need to find positive reinforcement wherever you can. I remember a speaking engagement I did in Alabama, telling the kids not to worry about making mistakes or failing, but to do everything with joy and excitement. One of the girls wrote me a letter thanking me. Her goal was to be a singer but she was thinking about quitting because she didn't feel she would make it. She said my words kept her singing, inspired her to keep going and stick with her goal. She said she wouldn't give up so easily again.

5. Set goals as a habit. How does setting goals become a way of life? You have to begin when you're young and pursue setting short term goals on a daily basis. Ask yourself, "What do I want to accomplish today? What can I do today that will help me tomorrow?" Then you do the same the next day and the next week. Do something each day that will help you reach the next day as a better person. This will keep you equipped to set and reach goals. If you have a daily agenda it will become part of your character. Keep these early goals realistic and within an arm's reach. If your early goals are small, they will allow you to build a solid foundation and increase your enthusiasm for pursuing them.

You may not like some of these early goals. Suppose your parents tell you to keep your room clean—okay, not your favorite task. Do it anyway, because it is important to learn how to be disciplined and organized. Accept the goal with enthusiasm even though you do not like it. Then, set a schedule to accomplish this goal and break it down. Perhaps you gather your dirty clothes one day, get your books in order the next, organize your CDs and DVDs the next and dust all your furniture the day after that. Try to make a game out of it, a challenge. Create your own excitement by asking yourself how you can make it enjoyable. This is a great way to generate enthusiasm for pursuing goals. Once you're enthusiastic, that's 80 percent of the battle. It keeps you motivated. All the while, you're creating a habit and that habit is pursuing your goals.

Remember, there are going to be times when you aren't getting the results you want and will feel you are losing that enthusiasm. You'll know when. You won't be excited about reaching the goal anymore. You may have good days and bad days. But if you start to hate every day, then it's time to change. If you keep your enthusiasm, you'll find a way to make progress. On those rare occasions where you begin to lose energy and don't see any more progress, go to the people who have been encouraging you and tell them what happened. Chances are they will tell you to get right back up on the horse, to set another goal and begin pursuing it immediately. Then, remember how you learned to make things fun. It can happen that way again. Sometimes we all pick a goal that isn't quite right for us and we have to abandon it and set another. But if you've made setting and reaching goals a habit, it will be easier to forget the one that didn't work and pursue the next one the same enthusiastic way.

6. Write down your goals. There are a number of reasons why you should always write down your goals. For one thing, you may think of something you feel you may want to do, then get busy with something else and forget about it. If you write it down immediately, you'll be reminded. Write down why you feel it's important to reach that goal and what you feel it is going to take to get there. As you write, you can also visualize yourself reaching it. That will keep you balanced. It also sometimes helps to put down a time line for short term goals. This will give your goals a structure. You don't want to spend too much time on something or less time than you should. That's where a time line will help. Make sure your timeline is realistic by checking it with an expert.

You can also write down a long term goal that you feel might be too difficult for you at that particular time. We all sometimes have dreams or visions of ourselves sometime in the future, but it's too soon. You may need another two or three years before the time is right and you can make a final decision. But if you write these thoughts and goals down, they will remain with you until you are ready to decide if this is really what you want.

It never hurts to write down your dreams and visions as goals. Sometimes if you write out a goal that is particularly difficult, that will ultimately help you to fight through to reach it. Then the next time you write one down that seems very difficult, you'll be reminded that you did it once before. Writing things down serves many purposes, none of which are more important than when your goals are realized on paper. When you write your goals down and you review them, you'll have a barometer of your success. This will motivate you even more.

Goals and Changes
You always have to be aware of changes in your life, your outlook, your dreams and your goals. Suppose your family moves to another city and you have to change schools. You now have a whole new group of friends. You have to be careful not to allow these changes to affect who you are. Being able to adjust to change is a huge asset.

When I tore the anterior cruciate ligament (ACL) in my knee, it was a huge adjustment for me. My goal every year was to play better than the year before. In this condition, I had to decide whether to retire or try to keep playing. I looked inside myself and realized my heart was still in the game. I wanted to play. I also knew I would have to work extra hard to "rehab" my knee after surgery. When I had to sit out with the injury, I was miserable. But my desire to play again was so strong that I did whatever it took. My goal changed from playing to getting ready to play again. This was an unexpected detour that took a major adjustment on my part. But my goal remained strong and I made it all the way back through hard, hard work, and by setting small realistic goals.

When you have a change or detour in your life you've got to keep a grip on your long term goals. You must ask yourself if you're willing to make changes, find the resources you need to move forward, and the confidence you need to persevere. In my case, I spoke to people who had a similar injury. I asked them how they dealt with it, and what they did when they ran into plateaus or they didn't improve enough. I asked them how they overcame their injury. Knowing what to expect ahead of time helped me tremendously. It took me nine months to get back on the court. A torn ACL is a devastating injury for an aging basketball player, but my goal was to return to the court and I took it up a notch to make that happen. When I played again after the injury, my dream was once again fulfilled.

So there may be all kinds of changes you have to deal with in life while keeping focused on your goals. If your goal involves sports, you have to be prepared for the changes caused by injury. Sometimes a bad injury can derail you permanently and you have to choose a different path. But if you push through it and are able to continue toward your goal it will be a great thing for you mentally. My dad used to say, "Learn the lessons of adjustment. Always be flexible." Changes can make you stronger and stretch you to new levels. Don't let your attitude keep you down.

Another change may be brought about by moving to a new city. You may find you suddenly don't have all the resources you had before. That's when you need discipline to continue what you started before you moved. If your goal is to pursue music and they don't have instruction at your new school, you'll have to find other ways to pursue your goal. Seek out new resources. There is always more than one way to accomplish something. Look at life as a journey. What you're going through at the moment is only part of that journey.

Don't let change scare you. Stay the course and continue to pursue your next goal and your ultimate dream. One of the values of setting goals is making your journey through life a great one. The short term goals we have talked about are all experiences on that journey. They will teach you about yourself and help you stay on the right road to completing the journey. Changes are always part of the equation. Embrace them!

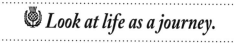 *Look at life as a journey.*

There will also be times when life will throw you a curve ball, creating another detour on your road to reaching a goal. For example, suppose you're in high school and pushing hard to get a college scholarship. Suddenly, a family crisis develops and you have to work after school and on weekends to help out. Family certainly has to come first. You may have to put some of your plans on a temporary hold. You can always get back on track later or find a way to divide your time without burning the candle at both ends. Follow your heart and make the best decision you can. I would never advise someone to neglect their family to pursue their own ends.

Setting goals is often about reassessing and self-evaluating. You sometimes have to look at what you enjoy as opposed to what captures your passion. Many things will catch your eye, but only a few will drive your heart. If you feel you can't live without something then pursue it, even if you aren't going to be the best. Go after what you value the most. Your goal can simply be to enjoy something at whatever level you happen to reach.

When you assess what you are doing, think about whether you are really having a good time. There are people who have jobs they're passionate about even though they might make more money doing something else. But they want that which gives them excitement and fuels their passion. It makes them feel like a better person. That's the key. Your goal doesn't always have to be something you're great at, only something you do well. However, it never hurts to keep trying to be better!

There are some kids who want to be great from a young age. They see themselves as a sports star or a popular actor on TV, or maybe a singer with one gold record after another. They always want to reach that next level. But if you want to reach the top, you've got to understand what goes with it, a great deal of hard work, discipline and sacrifice. And, it's not always easy to keep your life in balance.

If your goal involves being part of a team, you must think a bit differently. Setting goals always involves you as an individual. When you're part of a team, your goals change slightly. You have to think in terms of how you can be better in order to make your team better. Ask yourself if what you're doing is ultimately for the good of the team. As someone once said, "In order for the team to get better, I must first get better."

Goal setting is a simple; find something you like and are passionate about, and pursue it. Whether you succeed or suffer a setback, keep setting new goals, keep looking for things that strike your heart and ignite your passion. That keeps you alive and moving forward until you achieve the success you really want. By that time, you should know just how to pursue it. Life's curve balls are meant to help you thrive.

In summing up, here are some basic rules to remember when beginning and continuing to set and pursue goals. Once you understand them you should be ready to pursue your goals, no matter what they are.

1. Understand the goal you're setting.
2. Know what it will take to achieve that goal. Break it down into smaller pieces.
3. Once you know what you have to do, be willing, ready and disciplined to do it.
4. Find out the resources you'll need and where they are.
5. Learn the process. Understand the specific steps you need to take to accomplish your goal.
6. Don't hesitate to ask for help when you feel you need it.
7. Be willing to make the necessary sacrifices, some of which may be quite large.
8. Track and assess your progress, but don't lose patience.
9. Slow things down when necessary. Success doesn't happen overnight.
10. Always write your progress down. Review your accomplishments frequently.

These rules are very basic, but they worked for me. Remember to stay on course. That's the important thing. Once you begin setting goals as a youngster, keep it up. You will gain confidence to set larger and larger goals as you grow older. Ultimately, one of those goals will take you on the path to what you want to do most in life. Stick to the principles you learn now and you'll get there.

Many things will catch your eye, but only a few will drive your heart.

CHAPTER SIX
OVERCOMING ADVERSITY

Adversity. This isn't a word people welcome. According to the dictionary, it signifies misfortune and trouble. Unfortunately, none of us can escape encountering adversity at some point in our lives. When it's right there before you, the sooner you learn how to face it and ultimately overcome it, the sooner you'll continue to travel on a forward path in your life. Adversity comes in many forms—a mountain, a valley, an obstacle or opportunity—and in all shapes and sizes. You may encounter adversity at any time and at any age, and definitely more than once. But if you learn how to deal with it when you're young, you'll have a much easier time overcoming adversity when you're older.

In your formative years, adversity may come in the form of bullying, trying to belong, struggling with your grades, looking for the right kind of friends, problems at home or even with sports. Why is it so important to learn to deal with adversity? The answer is simple and frightening at the same time. Adversity can make or break you. If you begin running away from it early on, you'll be running the rest of your life. It's difficult to face adversity when you are young because you may not fully under-stand how your emotions work. Still, you must learn to embrace your problem, to use whatever adversity you encounter to become stronger and ultimately guide yourself in your chosen direction.

The reason my dad taught us over and over about building a strong foundation and having a great attitude, as well as developing a great work ethic, was because he knew life could throw some real curves at you. That was his way of preparing us to deal with adversity. He always told us: "Life is 10 percent what happens to you and 90 percent how you respond to it." A positive attitude will play a huge role in how you deal with the curve balls in your life. You always need someone to rely on. I was fortunate to have had my dad. Without his early teaching about attitude and mindset, I would have had a much more difficult time dealing with adversity.

All of us will have to face a major adversarial situation sooner or later.

My big challenge occurred when I wasn't recruited to play basketball at Auburn University, where my sister, Maeola was already a basketball star. I was told I wasn't good enough to even play until my junior year. Thanks to my dad's advice, I chose to embrace the toughest road. By facing that situation head on and working through it, I became a lot stronger, had more confidence, and elevated myself to a whole new level. If I had chosen the easier road and gone to a smaller school, I might have still been somewhat successful but probably not as successful as I became by embracing and accepting the Auburn University challenge. Choosing the rough road broadened and expanded me. In spite of the odds, I was able to overcome and reached the level I did as a basketball player. It truly helped define me. It was an outstanding benchmark in my life—overcoming that challenge and the adversity it presented opened the doors to future opportunities.

My Ride of A Lifetime

This is how I embraced the pain of adversity and conquered the hurt and fear. I knew I loved basketball. My sisters and brothers, especially, Maeola, played all the time. Even though I knew I was not as good as Maeola, I believed I could be as competitive. I shared her triumphs—her high school basketball championships, and her recruitment and acceptance to a Southeastern Conference school. I was impressed by the way the universities fought over my sister, making great offers that would help her change her life and finish her education. Auburn University and many other schools even paid for her airline tickets to tour the schools. Few of us had never flown before, and this was a sure sign that the universities believed in her skills and wanted her on their teams.

Since I was one year younger than Maeola, and also helped lead my high school team to two championships, I was certain I would get similar treatment and follow in her footsteps. That did not happen. Instead, I was rebuffed and told I wasn't good enough. What's worse—no other university recruited me. They all felt that I wasn't worth the investment. I was devastated. Even though I played my heart out, no school wanted me. I felt dejected and angry. I was so discouraged, I lost my interest in the game and almost quit. But Dad wouldn't let me wallow in my sorrow. He encouraged me to call the Auburn University coach and ask him if they were going to give me a visit to the school. I followed Dad's direction and called. The coach told me that they would put me on a Greyhound Bus in about a week. I was so excited to be going to Auburn University even if it meant riding a bus for eight hours. I sat in that bus with no food in my stomach. But, I had joy in my heart because I was on my way to the dream I had prayed for.

When I arrived, I was invited to dinner at the coach's home with my sister Maeola. We had a very enjoyable dinner with his family and friends. After dinner, the coach called me into his home office and said: "Ruthie, I'm sorry I had you come here. We should have never had you take the trip. This is too high a level of play for you. You will probably not even make the travel team, so you may be miserable here. It would be tough for your sister to watch you agonize, so we suggest you go to another school. We will try to help you get accepted elsewhere. But, because we promised your parents to help you get a scholarship to finish your studies here, we'll honor that. You may not even get a chance to play until your third year."

The joy in my heart became a deep sadness in my soul. Now, I had a decision to make. Should I stay or leave? I felt ambushed, confused and let down. I couldn't even respond. I was speechless. My basketball dream was fading away. I just sat there—dejected, angry and empty.

Even though the coach tried to console me, I really didn't hear a thing. This was my only chance to play, no other university showed interest. All I could think of was my dad—I longed for his counsel because I didn't know what to do or how to feel. I hurt so badly, I lost my appetite. I don't remember the ride back to my home in McLain. But, as soon as I got there, I talked to my dad.

"Dad, they don't want me," I cried. "Daughter," he said, "you don't have to own other people's perceptions of you. Be yourself. Live by your principles of faith, shore up your attitude, and go forward. I believe in you. I've watched you in the backyard. I've seen you develop your stamina. They just don't know you have what it takes. Stay there and show them what you got. I believe in your work ethic. God is not going to go out there and run sprints for you. You have to outwork people and keep your attitude in check. Let your actions and your strength speak for you. Find the opening to get through and deal with the situation. Daughter, adversity is just a part of life. Let these adversities teach you and make you strong. Whatever blessing God has for you, nobody can take away. Focus on your attitude and your mindset. It will pull you through it all."

His encouraging words made me feel so good, it erased my doubts. I was ready to fight for my chance. In fact, I was so competitive and strong not only did I make the team in my freshman year, the coach used my skill and work ethics as a standard for other players. I beat all odds and started playing on the team in six weeks. I had become an asset to the team by not letting adversity derail me.

How you deal with the cards you are sometimes dealt is very important. You won't know if you don't try to overcome adversity. When I decided to go to Auburn University despite the coach telling me I wouldn't play, it taught me a lot about myself and my inner strength. I wouldn't have known that about myself if I didn't embrace that mountain and then set out to climb it. I kept saying I know I can do that. It felt good then, and it still feels good to look back and think about it today.

Overcoming adversity isn't always easy. You've got to learn some basic lessons early so you develop the confidence and positive mental attitude you will need to succeed. So let's start by looking at some of the adversities you might encounter in your early years.

....

🌣 *A setback is a setup for a comeback.*

....

Loss of a Loved One

Losing a loved one is difficult. A younger child who loses a parent, sibling or even a best friend must find a way to grieve. If this happens to you, don't ignore it. Trying to be a tough superhero, acting as if it doesn't bother you, won't work. Try writing about it. That can help relieve anxiety as well as allow you to express your feelings. When you do this, be true to how you feel. If you're angry, express it. Then try to latch on to something that is positive and good. That will help you to find a way to remember the good times. It will also help to keep that person alive in your mind and heart.

You can also find other ways to keep that person alive for you. If you lose someone who loved football, just getting a football to keep will help. If that person loved animals, maybe you can become an advocate for animal safety and get a pet to care for. When my mom passed away, I remembered the last time I saw her I touched her left hand and told her how pretty her hands were. After that, each time I came onto the court to start a game I always touched my own hand so she'd know I was thinking of her. I constantly speak of my dad when I talk before a group, and I feel that he goes everywhere with me.

Avoid anger and practice forgiveness. Otherwise, adversities like loss of a loved one will eat at you. It is really difficult to rise if someone you love is killed in an accident. It may be difficult to forgive the person who caused the accident, but forgiveness is the key to your own peace of mind. You can't bring that person back, so you have to be sure that these negative feelings won't consume and overtake you. Sometimes there is so much anger that you may need counseling or some other type of professional help. If you can't rid yourself of angry or negative feelings, then getting help is a good idea.

Everyone experiences death at some point in their lives and it is very hard to prepare for it. Unfortunately, it's part of life. Fortunately, we can hold on to the good memories. The fact that you can lose someone makes it important not to take loved ones for granted. Tell them you love them and treat them right so there will be no guilt if that person passes. Life is too short to hold on to grudges against someone. If you do lose a loved one who wanted the best for you, then continue to strive for the things you both wanted. That, too, is another positive way to honor them.

Ruthie in action

Peer Pressure

Bolton facing a little peer pressure from opponent. Close caption]
Everyone wants to fit in. This is a statement virtually no young person
will deny. Along those same lines, no one wants to be ridiculed. But you
have to understand that kids are going to say hurtful things. Remember,
those who are saying things about you are really saying things about
themselves. They're usually insecure and unhappy. That said, you still
have to speak against what you are being told. If they say, for example,
that you're stupid, you should tell them point blank that you are not. Just
maintain authority and coolness within yourself. If you hear something
over and over again and don't say anything, you may begin to believe it.

Peer pressure can create major adversity in your life. You've got to
resist doing the wrong thing. Because people want to fit in, sometimes
they allow themselves to be led down the wrong path. If you're trying
to fit in with a group that's doing the wrong things, then find some new
friends. If, for example, your so-called "friends" are trying to get you to
take drugs, then they are not really your friends. They just want to see
you destroy yourself because that's what they're doing to themselves.
Even if you have made some mistakes, it's never too late to walk away
and change your life. You can always find new friends who are engaged
in positive activities.

Because peer pressure is often very powerful, it can also be a positive
experience. If your friends are telling you to study more, to work harder
on the basketball court or to practice a musical instrument more, then
the peer pressure is positive. Remember to always look in the mirror
to see who you really are. Remember that peer pressure can be a major

distraction that can hurt you, or a positive force for the good. Choose the good. You'll reap greater rewards in your life.

All kids are curious. If you tell them don't eat that particular apple from that tree, that's the one they'll often want. I tell kids that they're going to make mistakes, but that's part of learning who they really are. So, remember to make you own decisions. Don't settle or surrender to what people say. If you move off track, make it your business to get back on track. You'll never be perfect, but you can bounce back, no matter what you've done. Just don't give your life away to negative influences. Then, you'll end up a person that no one cares about. Parents and teachers can be sources of inspiration. Talk to them honestly.

Look at yourself as a leader. If you're with a group, take the responsibilities of a leader. Every youth needs to think he or she is valuable and that's why I listen carefully when they talk to me. You do that and you'll find something positive in each person. Then you can nurture the positive side of your life with supportive people. Negative peer pressure won't win if you stay occupied by doing positive things.

Talk to your parents if you are pressured to do bad things, or find a teacher, a coach or a clergyman, someone you can reach out to that will listen and understand what you are going through. Everyone needs someone to be there for them to act as a sounding board. It is even better when the person understands the pressures they're experiencing. Some kids join gangs just because they need to belong to something. Some youth feel they have nothing else better to do. That's why sports and other after school programs are so important. They give people positive challenges and encourage discipline and structure. These programs help young people overcome the adversity of negative peer pressure.

Bullying

It's apparent to anyone who has been bullied that it doesn't feel good. No one should have to put up with bullying. Someone who is the target of a bully or bullies should reach out to their teachers, the principal and their parents. There's no shame in asking for help. If the bully is picking on you, he or she will also pick on someone else. Go to someone in authority and let your parents know what is happening. This is very important. Many parents and others in authoritative positions don't always know the degree to which bullying is happening.

You must remember that bullies act the way they do out of their own insecurity. It can only help if you are secure and confident, and know just who you are. But at the same time you have to find the courage to stand up for yourself. Bullies are often bored with school and some also have problems at home. They intimidate and control others to make themselves feel powerful.

When I was bullied, I was embarrassed to tell anyone at first. Finally,

I stood up to the girl who was bullying me and, believe it or not, she apologized. It turned out that she was insecure and really wanted to be my friend. She knew I was shy then and took my kindness for weakness. Bullies, on the whole, have very little self-respect and may not be happy. But a bully can also turn his or her life around if someone begins rooting for them, encourages them, and gives them respect and a more meaningful connection to caring people.

As with so many other things, if you find yourself being bullied write about it. Jot down how you feel, how you plan to deal with it and whether it is affecting your schoolwork and other aspects of your life. You'll feel better and you'll also create a picture of what is happening with you. That way, you'll have a record of everything and can more accurately describe it when you seek help.

Bullying can be a huge adversity in a young person's life. It must be overcome. Get help if you must, but also stand up for yourself and maintain a strong self-image. You can't let a bully win. Neither can you keep running from them. Otherwise, you live in fear and become something less than you can be. Every adversity that you overcome makes you stronger and wiser, and gives you more energy and stamina to go through life successfully.

....

"Holding on to anger is like grasping a hot coal with the intent of throwing it at someone else."
—Buddha

....

Anger

Anger is a very strong emotion; It can be both positive and negative. It can be positive if it spurs you to work harder and achieve more.

When it is negative, it can tear you down. It's all right to say, "I'm angry," but it's how you deal with or manage your anger that's important. If someone says, for instance, that you're not good enough at something and you get angry, it can help you, but only if you say, "I'm going to show you I'm good enough," and start to work even harder to reach your goal. Then you are making anger work for you. But if you allow it to consume and overtake you, then anger can jeopardize your future. You can easily become a prisoner of anger. It starts with one negative event and quickly leads to a series of negative events that get you into deeper trouble.

Learn how to manage anger. Anger provides warnings, or it may be a sign that your safety is endangered. Dr. Bill Knaus, psychologist and author of more than twenty books, tells us:

Unlike a natural anger, that is defense against real danger, ego anger froths with irrational demands, recurs and lingers. That's the enemy. When anger rules reason, disaster may follow in the form of physical violence and relationship losses. When expressing anger, people may tune into your emotion and ignore your ideas. If you seethe for years, over one thing or another, you risk coronary heart disease. If you are in an anger trap, change course. Exercise your reason. You are then likely to move like a well-tuned race car that reason steers and emotion fuels. You can do this with confident composure. With confident composure, you recognize that you can directly command only yourself, and you choose to do so. You don't demand that the world change for you and you don't need it to. With this softer but stronger view, you can better influence the controllable events that take place around you. (Bill Knaus, *Psychology Today*, April 2001.)

Ruthie never let anger take control of her and absorbed the positivity from controlling her anger.

You can become angry for a variety of reasons. You might be late for an appointment or event because the traffic is bad. Or you might be sitting on the bench, in a sport when you feel you should be playing. The traffic jam is something you can't really do anything about. It happens. But if you're sitting on the bench you have to ask yourself what you can do to play more. Talk to the coach. Be confident and composed. Ask what you have to do to get better, and then work hard toward it. If you just sit and feel sorry for yourself, you are letting the anger control and consume you. Then it will affect other areas of your life, such as slacking off with your schoolwork.

It's also important to forgive yourself for being angry and to ask what triggered the anger. You aren't perfect—no one is—and you are allowed to make some mistakes. No matter what you've done, there will still be the opportunity to turn things around, to redeem yourself and fix what has been broken. You also have to feel you're important enough that you deserve better. You need to remember that you are special.

People remain angry because they haven't dealt with it. They may have one big pity party and become angrier and angrier. That can seal their fate. When you meet people like that you can hear it in their voice. In many cases, people like that are angry at themselves. I've spent many long hours talking about and dealing with anger in the program that I present at schools. I know that anger can cheat you of the right to have a joyful and happy life. When someone is angry all the time, they have really lost control of themselves.

One method to rid yourself of anger is something I call FRE, standing for free, as in freeing yourself of the anger. It works like this.

> **F** is for *forgive*. You must learn to not only forgive yourself, but to forgive the person or persons who caused the anger, even before they ask for forgiveness. If they don't ask, you must still find the power to forgive. You must refuse to let people hurt you by making you angry. If you don't forgive, you're giving anger too much power to control your emotions.

> **R** is for *release*. You need to find a way to release your anger. For me, exercise always worked. I would run, ride a bike, and play ball, anything to relax my body. You can achieve some release by writing down your thoughts or talking about it with someone you trust and respect. You can also cry. Never think that shedding tears is a sign of weakness. It's simply another form of releasing.

> **E** is for *empowerment*. Don't just sweep things under the rug and pretend you aren't angry when you really are. If you express yourself in a positive manner you're being true to yourself. And that's another important quality when trying to overcome the adversity of anger.

Controlling Your Anger

Because everyone becomes angry at some point in their lives, you have to be ready to control that anger. Those around you will learn from your actions. I was angry with the way I was treated in my final year with the Monarchs, but I had learned long ago to always be a team player. I knew I couldn't allow my personal situation to affect the team. One of my teammates, who knew what was happening, said she would never have known what I was going through by watching the way I interacted with my teammates.

At the time, I had a coach who wanted to cut me from the team. I wasn't allowed to play. Because of my long and successful career, I thought he should have given me the option of playing because it was my last year. It turned into one of the toughest experiences of my life and taught me a lot about myself. Though I was very angry, I didn't want my anger to destroy me and what I had built over the years. I'm glad I went through the experience and handled it effectively. If I was vindictive, I could have become a disruptive force for the entire team. You have to learn how to find closure with these situations in a positive way.

This wasn't easy and it took me months to really deal with it. I was always loyal to the organization. The coach barely played me. He wanted a different type of team, and said that he wanted the team to go in a different direction. I had a choice to retire or to stay with the organization as an employee. There were other teams interested in me. The Monarchs had offered me a terrible contract. Fortunately, my dad had prepared me for situations like this. I chose to retire, which was somewhat bittersweet, because I wasn't ready to retire. But I knew God would open another door for me. Controlling my anger in this difficult situation taught me a lot about my character.

Your life is too important to live in anger. You have to manage it the right way and make a conscious choice to do this. There are many people behind bars today because of uncontrollable anger. These individuals didn't try to control their anger. Instead, they let it go and wound up in jail. So if you don't begin controlling anger early, there's a chance your freedom will be taken away, and no one wants that.

Because dealing with anger is such an important part of overcoming adversity, let's review the steps to take from the time you first feel anger building up within you.

1. Identify, as best you can, why you are angry.
2. Try to figure out why you allowed the situation to make you so angry that you can't function normally. You may not know why.
3. Ask yourself what you can do to lose or lessen the anger. Do you need to talk to someone? Do you need counseling? Who can I trust that will listen to my feelings?
4. Write down all your thoughts about becoming so angry.
5. Cry if you must. It can cleanse the soul and is a positive way to release your feelings.
6. Express what is happening. Acknowledge what it is. Then be true to yourself about it.
7. Learn to forgive. If you can't forgive, the anger will remain. So forgive both yourself and others.
8. Find a way to lose the anger and put yourself back on a positive path. Otherwise, the anger will control you. Anger is an adversity you have to overcome.

Use Your Inner Strength

Adversity and tough times reveal your character. When you fight through adversity, you strengthen your character and keep moving forward. My brother, Paul, used to say a setback is a setup for a comeback. Setbacks can motivate you to work even harder. It's all a matter of attitude and approach.

Adversity helps you tap into the power within, your inner strength. Anytime you get past any kind of adversity, you'll find yourself getting stronger and stronger. Don't underestimate your strength. You must embrace the challenges before you. You're going through adversity for a reason and you have to feel the situation will make you better. There's a learning experience in everything. Look for it. Lose your fear and hang in there. Keep thinking that you can overcome the obstacles in your path to become a stronger and better person. Remember, adversity prepares you for something greater, for what you will ultimately become.

What If You Want to Quit

Adversity is never easy, nor is learning how to take a punch and getting back up again. So while you may know all the ways in which to overcome a difficult situation, an adversity can sometimes seem overwhelming. Don't feel bad if you suddenly want to quit. Everyone feels like quitting sometimes. That's why half the battle is not quitting, no matter what. If you fall down seven times, but get up eight times, then you're winning the battle.

To keep yourself from quitting you have to keep looking forward, see the value in what you're trying to overcome, and remind yourself of your purpose. It's easy to lose sight of that. When I think about my purpose, it gives me strength and that extra push to keep going. If, for example, you're on a sports team but not playing much you may want to quit. But maybe you promised yourself you wouldn't quit, or promised your parents you'd stick it out. Or maybe you love the game and want to go to the next level. You can use all these things to find the strength that will keep you pushing forward. If you quit, you'll never have a chance.

If you're finding adversity in something for which you once had true passion, that alone is a good reason not to quit. Just think about the passion you had before things went wrong. Remember, not everything you want to do will be easy. It's hard to achieve some things, even if you enjoy doing it. You have to reawaken your passion. Square your shoulders to adversity. Defy it. Ask it to show you what it has. Then take it on by the horns. Having a strong attitude and drive gives you the resilience to bounce back like a rubber band. The harder you pull, the stronger you'll bounce back. If you want to get up, you can. Find the value in your struggle with adversity and use your will to keep going.

The key is developing the habit of getting back up to pursue your dreams. You must recognize and understand early that it's all right to make mistakes. You aren't perfect. It may take you awhile to get back up the first time, but that's fine. You need patience when you come upon adversity and get knocked down. You have to value yourself enough to know you deserve to get up and continue to move forward. It was a very tough blow when I didn't make the Olympic team the first time I tried out. But I got up, worked harder and harder and by the time the next Olympics came, I was ready and well-equipped.

Ruthie Bolton and the Olympic Team stand in the Oval Office with President Bill Clinton before the Olympics of 1996

Going through adversity alone is tough. You're more likely to give up if you don't have a support group, someone to lean on. One of the main punches I took was when I wasn't recruited for college, but my dad gave me the confidence to keep working to put my dream back in reach. Every time I hit a roadblock, I would call my dad because I always knew he had strong shoulders for me to lean on.

If you're taking one punch after another, it is even more difficult. Then it becomes a matter of refusing to give up. Quitting is the easy way out. Every time you get back on your feet it's a new day and a new opportunity. The game always starts at zero to zero. So at the beginning, you always have a chance to win. Spring is coming, no matter how tough the winter has been. Remember that if you fall down and want to quit, getting up is part of growing and developing. You have the power to get back up. You can get up. Don't quit.

If you fall down seven times, but get up eight times, then you're winning the battle.

Remaining Humble

Remaining humble is an important quality, but perhaps never more so than when adversity strikes. You can't become cocky and feel that nothing will challenge or stop you. If you get that way, you can easily be caught by surprise. You must learn to be prepared for the unexpected. Sports are a perfect example. You must be humble and respect your opponent. By doing that and paying attention to small details, you will be more successful.

Staying humble is a wise thing, because you recognize that you're not invincible. I have a friend who is addicted to alcohol. He's been sober for 17 years. I've gone to Alcoholics Anonymous meetings with him and he still says his name, followed by "And I'm an alcoholic." He says you have to stay humble and be aware that adversity can overtake you in a minute. One drink and you can fall again. You can't take anything for granted.

When I was on the Olympic teams we remained humble when it came to our opponents. It helped us to stay focused. When you take the other team for granted, you can lose easily by underestimating their power. Don't ever think you're too big and that nothing bad can happen. Adversity may be lurking around the next corner. As soon as you get cocky and think you have it made, you can hit the wall. It's fine to be confident, but never take things for granted.

I practice humility daily. I know I'm not indispensable and can run into issues at any time. Adversity is always there, so you must be prepared for it. When you remain humble, there's much less chance of adversity ambushing you. It is one thing to remain positive, but don't think adversity won't ever happen. Challenges will be sure to come. But if you're humble, you're more likely to see the warning signs; you are more likely to be prepared.

....

🌣 *Spring is coming, no matter how tough the winter has been.*

....

Working Harder and Smarter

Whenever adversity stands before you, prepare to work even harder because the usual effort may not be enough. Again, you have to look at this as an opportunity to grow and become a better person. It will give you a work ethic that can last forever. Most young people, especially the youngest kids, don't like adversity. They often fear it, and that makes facing it even more difficult. The trick is to develop the mindset to work through adversity. Without it, you'll become even more fearful of adversity as you get older. Too many people simply don't see the value in old-fashioned hard work.

There's an old adage in sports that also applies to taking on adversity, "No pain, no gain." You may not be crazy about these kinds of challenges, but take them on and you'll not only become wiser, but stronger, and that will prepare you for so much more in life.

If you run away early, you'll always run away. Many people just don't see the value in hard work when, in reality, they should embrace it. It's a win-win situation when you work hard to overcome adversity—especially when you work smarter on the right things.

I once attended a youth conference where the logo was a butterfly spreading its wings. A caterpillar has to struggle to become a butterfly just as a person has to struggle sometimes to work harder at overcoming adversity. But that's part of the growth process. Always remember, success is just around the corner from adversity. Athletes always experience soreness when getting into shape. Their bodies are adjusting to the use of new muscle fibers. In developing a work ethic, your mind is also adjusting to a new way of thinking, but you'll be acquiring a mindset that will never leave you. I've seen many kids who aren't afraid and I know they already have a character trait that will help them in every aspect of their lives.

Those who are not working to tackle adversity, need to reach out and make themselves available to someone who can give advice and encourage them. If you don't reach out you'll find yourself in a lonely and scary place. Just calling my dad and hearing his voice always gave me so much strength. So it's important to have people like that in your life. Otherwise, you may lose your center of stability. You may stop wanting to be with your friends, lose your appetite to eat well, stop watching your favorite shows, or stop spending your time doing positive things. You may just want to sit alone, which is not healthy at any age. Those things usually indicate that your depressed—an unproductive slump.

As a coach, I've watched some players change. Gradually, they stop working as hard. Their personalities cease to be as engaging. When I approach a kid who is acting this way, I'll often find he or she is dealing with some heavy issues, maybe at home, maybe at school. There's usually some kind of adversity that they are simply not facing. That's when I let them know I'm there to talk. It's very important for a leader to identify and deal with a behavioral change because depression is very bad for young kids.

Sometimes adversity will cause young people to blame themselves, to think they made a mistake. I've always looked at it this way. There is no such thing as mistakes. If you learn from them, then it becomes a growing process. Mistakes can turn into life lessons and so can overcome adversity. Don't let people tell you that you are a failure when something temporarily derails you. Keep telling yourself, "I am someone special and I have things I want to do." Always let the positive dominate the negative. Feed your passion. Practice your faith.

Dealing With Adversity Can Define You

Make it your goal to get past the adversity. You'll find a great deal of self-satisfaction when you fight through something and overcome it. You'll feel so good about yourself; your confidence will double. That's the reward for all your hard work and for sticking with it. Now you'll be ready to move on to the next level with a fearless mentality and an increased drive. You'll become smarter about how to handle the next adverse action. When I went to Auburn University and became an impact player my first year, I was so proud. Imagine that! They said I couldn't make the teams. It's an amazing feeling when you've overcome a major adversity. It makes many other smaller obstacles seem easy. It gives you a sharper foundation, and drives you to keep improving.

In addition, other people will respect you more. You'll become a more positive role model for others. When I was living with a family in Italy, the mother saw me going to the gym and running regularly. She was so impressed by my dedication that she began running and, at the age of 40, began competing in marathons. In fact, both she and her friend did it. They said they were encouraged by my perseverance.

Ruthie's Italian family came to see her play in the 1996 Olympics held in Atlanta and the 2000 Olympics held in Australia.

When you have resilience and embrace adversity, you inspire other people. That's the heart of a true champion. It's a beautiful thing when you see someone getting better just by watching you.

Steps to Overcoming Adversity

As with anything that is difficult in life, there is no one set formula for overcoming adversity. But there are some general rules that will work for anyone who is willing to follow them and has a strong enough foundation and mindset to stay the course. So let's go over them once more.

1. Address the situation directly. That means admitting to the adversity that's in front of you. You can't do anything until you define the problem.
2. Ask yourself if you really want to change. What must you do to resolve the issues?
3. Figure out exactly what you must do to make it happen. If necessary, seek out advice from someone you trust and find encouragement. Practice harder and smarter to give you that extra bit of confidence.
4. Dedicate yourself to the work that must be done. Develop a routine schedule and do the work. Discipline yourself. Persevere. Keep going forward no matter what. Things don't change overnight. So hang in there and keep from being discouraged. Take replenishing breaks with family and uplifting friends.
5. Celebrate and analyze your success. You are going to find more adversity in the future, but now you know what must be done to overcome it. You've become even stronger.

If you follow these rules and persist, you can overcome almost anything. It won't always be easy. Roadblocks and obstacles are always going to be there. When you know you can overcome adversity, the rewards become greater as you grow and succeed knowing you have the inner strength to win. This is the mark of a champion!

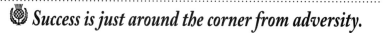 *Success is just around the corner from adversity.*

CHAPTER SEVEN
BEATING THE ODDS

Nobody likes to hear the word "NO." Adults don't like it and neither do children. With young children, the word means they cannot do something they want to do. They might be too young to understand the reason. All they know is that they want to do it and someone with authority is saying, *No, you can't.* For older children and adults, the word NO implies you have limits. So that simple little two-letter word can be discouraging, deflating, strip you of confidence, and make you fearful of failing. That's why it's so important to learn early on ways to beat the odds by turning a NO into a resounding YES!

There are many aspects to the word NO, some of it is directly linked to items in the previous chapter. That's because many of the same principles for success apply here, things such as strength of character, a willingness to work hard, a positive mindset, passion and drive. So when you read this chapter you may be tempted to say, "Hey, I've heard this before." Well, you have heard it before and you'll hear it again. Any time you are looking for a successful and positive life, you'll hear many of the same things because they contain the ingredients you'll need to keep moving forward. And the word NO has the ability to stop you in your tracks.

Looking back, I don't think I fully realized that NO could be turned into YES until my senior year in high school. That's when it seemed destiny was saying no, that we wouldn't win the state championship. We were trailing with time running short. But after our coach reminded us of how far we had come and asked us to dig down deep for a final push, we went out and won the game. The state championship was ours! We had literally turned NO into YES and it was a beautiful experience, the first of many for me. It taught me to think that there can be something positive behind a NO. Therefore, don't accept NO so easily. You can find a way to turn it into a YES. You may not know where it is going to come from or how it will happen, but once you do it, you'll have the strength to seek out the ways to turn a negative into a positive event.

On the flip side, once you accept NO and are fearful of moving beyond it, then you'll tend to accept it again and again without question. That will not only make you afraid to fail, but afraid to dream, as well. If you accept NO you'll be settling for the things other people tell you. You cannot allow other people's words to dictate who you are or what you can become. Do that, and the negatives coming from other people will hold you down, and that can suck the life out of you.

Remember, other people don't know what is inside of you. They don't know the extent of your character, skills, drive or passion. Many people are simply naysayers and discourage almost anyone. That's why, if you feel you want more, you cannot simply accept someone telling you no, you can't do it. Or no, you're not good enough. Or worse yet, no, you'll never become good enough. You must believe that there is more for you out there. You have a right to go beyond NO and seek out and find your YES! The power lies within you not within the naysayer.

No to Young Kids

The first time young children hear the word no, it will probably come from their parents. Obviously, children should obey just as they should obey all authority figures. In the majority of cases, parents are on your side. So if parents say no, you have to trust their judgment. Remember, most parents want you to succeed and want you to be safe and stay out of trouble. My parents said no to so much when I was young. There were places we couldn't go, things we couldn't do and we often couldn't understand why. But boundaries can be good and, at a young age, you simply have to trust your leaders—your parents.

When you're young, you are simply not wise enough to make certain decisions. You may not understand why your parents are saying no. Basically, parents are trying to guide you through those early years and give you a foundation. Saying no to certain requests is almost standard operation procedure when you're young. Once you're older, most parents will begin to give you more leeway and if they say no, will explain their reasoning more fully. So when parents say no, respecting their decision is generally a good idea. If you disagree, try to explain your side of the story with passion, and patience.

Your parents make decisions for you when you're young. It's typically best to accept their leadership and learn from them. They are giving you boundaries, teaching you to accept responsibility and to respect authority. So you have to keep trusting their guidance until you reach that point where you can ask more productive questions and encourage them to explain. My dad began explaining more according to our age. He would provide more complex explanations to a 15-year-old than an 8-year-old.

My mom would tell us we couldn't go swimming and we never quite understood why. Finally, we learned that she had lost a brother from drowning and was very wary of allowing her children to swim in deep water. Therefore, she had a reason for saying no. When we finally got older, she started letting us go, first the girls, then the boys—but only for an hour. Our parents were concerned about our safety and that's understandable—they did not want us to get hurt. We respected it when we were young and understood it when we were older.

Pretty soon all kids reach a point where they want to decide what clothes they want to wear and whether they want to play soccer or basketball. They want to choose their own friends. When you reach that stage, your parents may still say no to some things. By then you'll be asking why and they, for the most part, will give you a reason. You may not agree and have a right to ask why not, but they are still your parents. Chances are, however, that if you want to work toward something positive and are following the rules and regulations around the house and at school, your parents will say yes. When you show how responsible you can be in one area (for example keeping your room clean) parents will usually say yes to giving you more responsibility in another area.

Ruthie's nieces and nephews

Once you begin having dreams and ambitions you have to begin making more of your own decisions about how to turn NO into YES. When the colleges said no to me, telling me my basketball skills weren't developed enough, especially in comparison to my sister, Maeola, I had a big decision to make. I knew that Maeola was born with more raw talent. She was gifted and it wasn't difficult for her to impress people with her skills. It was much more difficult for me. I had to work harder

104

and figure out just what I had to do to reach that level. If I wasn't willing and determined to turn that NO into YES, by working harder and smarter on my skillset, it could have ended for me in high school.

It can also be difficult for young people to accept NO from someone outside the house. If your peers say no, you can't go with us; you are going to feel some rejection. But remember, if there are kids who don't like you or don't want you with them there will also be a lot of others who will want to hang out with you and go places with you. So when kids say no, don't ever think there is something wrong with you. You are somebody and you are special. Find your own special group.

Now let's look at some of the others aspects of hearing the word NO and how you can decidedly turn it into a YES.

No As a Personal Challenge

I have always looked at NO as a personal challenge, a reason to work harder. So in that sense, when someone tells you no, immediately use it as motivation. There is a challenge before you and you are now going to work to overcome it. When I wasn't getting recruiting letters from colleges they were telling me, in effect, that no, you aren't good enough. In this case, not only was my basketball career at stake, but the chance for a paid education as well. So this was one time when I would do anything and everything to turn NO into YES.

My dad told me not to accept the NO, but he also said don't take it personally. I had to ask myself if it was worth the struggle and the time it would take to convince them they were wrong. I was feeling rejection, hurt and disappointment, but I refused to surrender. I was willing to do whatever was necessary. It is a bit scary to start down that road, but when you have someone in your corner it makes it easier. I had my dad. He believed in me and told me, flat out, not to accept NO. I trusted him and he would explain as clear as day why I should keep going. He would tell me not to be angry with the university for saying no, just to prove them wrong.

If you don't have a dad like mine as you grow and develop, you should seek out other people to encourage you. It's much more difficult to do it alone. You always need someone to help you when you reach a crossroads—a teacher, coach, older sibling, a relative such as an aunt or uncle—someone to help pull you up when you need it the most. It's always better to surround yourself with people who encourage you. There's someone out there for everyone. In my case it was a parent, which was great.

If you aren't lucky enough to have a parent who can serve this role, seek people who you know are in your corner when you don't know which way to go. It's sometimes very tough to overcome a NO by yourself. At the time I wasn't recruited, my sister, Maeola still believed in me. We were very close. So it was family who always picked me up at a crossroads. If you play a sport, your coach may take on that role. Coaches play a huge role in kids' lives. If you don't play sports, you'll still find that person somewhere.

Look at NO as a challenge, something to be overcome. Once you learn about the ingredients you need to overcome a NO, they will serve you well the rest of your life.

Fear of Failure

Not wanting to fail is a natural thing for anyone, so it's not surprising that so many people, young and old, fear it. Everyone wants to be successful. When you are very young you want to please your parents. Later, you want everyone to think you've done well. Everyone has to learn early that they aren't perfect and will make mistakes. It is okay as long as you learn from them. So don't beat yourself up if you fail, but don't readily accept it, either. Every time you hear the word NO, a sense of failure comes with it. This is something you must learn to deal with.

It all begins with the right mindset. *I'm going to try hard and if I don't succeed I'm going to try even harder.* That's the kind of thinking that gives you the confidence to keep going. It's tough initially. You may fail, but you can't fear it. Look at failure as just a detour en route to the place where you are headed. If you want to achieve, you can't give up. If you're afraid to fail, it makes everything more difficult and puts a great deal of pressure on you.

As you turn NO into YES more often you become confident and energized. It was that way for me on the basketball court. I wanted to please the people watching me and always gave maximum effort. People watching appreciated that. When I went to Auburn University, failure wasn't an option. That was my mindset and the more success I had the more confident I became. Because of that I never stopped giving that 100 percent-plus effort. Once you stop trying, it's difficult to keep your confidence up. Having confidence allows you to learn from every NO, from every roadblock you encounter.

You also have to remember that there will be times when NO will remain NO. You can't turn every NO into YES. But in the process of trying, you're going to learn about yourself. You are building character through those tough times and if, at the end of the day, it's still NO, you can look in the mirror and know you put in the effort. In fact, there are times when NO can't be turned into a YES. This will only make you stronger. Your hard work and dedication won't be in vain. You just have to go in a direction where you can turn a negative into a positive.

If you fail to turn a NO into YES several times, you may want to give up. That's when you have to tighten your boot strings even more and dig down just a little deeper. Think of it this way. Whenever it rains and storms there's still going to be another beautiful day coming. Or no matter how much it snows or how cold it is, another spring is just around the corner. By the same token, you have to know there's a YES coming. Again, surround yourself with people who will encourage you. Then it doesn't matter how many times you fall down, but how many times you get up. What's most important is what you do when you get up. If you get up with a purpose, that will drive you even closer to success.

Hearing the word NO never feels good. One of the worst for me was when I didn't get invited to try out for the National team after Auburn University had made it to the Final Four. I was at the top of my game as a collegian and couldn't understand why they said no, why they didn't have enough respect to invite me to the trials. I felt it was a slap in my face. That left me with a decision. Do I stay mad and keep saying it isn't fair? Well, life isn't always fair. I wanted a YES, but the coaches were saying NO. Players who were not invited could pay their own way to the tryout, but making the team that way is difficult. They have a set of players (the ones invited) they will keep their eyes on. In other words, the coaches had a preconceived notion of who should be on the team and I wasn't one of them.

Ruthie and Nikki McCray proudly display their 1996 Olympic gold medals

Once again my dad advised me to follow my passion and if I had the money, then go. He also told me not to be afraid to fail. Instead, go prove them wrong for not inviting you. The odds were not in my favor. They invited 50 players and then picked two teams with 25 total players. There were about 100 paying their own way. I was in the pool of players who shouldn't have been there. But I worked harder and harder every practice session. At the end of the third day they had a list of names that made it and mine was there! Needless to say, I was thrilled. I felt I had already turned NO into YES by going and not being afraid to fail. Because I made the team, the money I spent to get there was given back to me. I was the only player picked from the group who had paid their own way. This was one time I not only turned NO into YES, but also turned it into GOLD; because we went on to win the 1996 gold medal. We became Olympic champions!

I moved to a whole new level of play simply because I refused to surrender. As my dad said, "Make it hard for them to say no." And that's just what I did. I turned the tables on them. But being able to do that didn't happen overnight. It took some setbacks and other rejections to reach that point, to give me the drive to excel in tough situations. I wasn't afraid to fail. Dad always said, "When you give it your all, you don't really fail. The best you can do is the best you can do, and that isn't really failure. It's when you stop without really trying that you do the most damage to yourself." Don't ever stop when you think you can win!

Being Competitive

Being competitive is a mindset. It's going toe to toe with your opponent and saying show me what you got. That opponent doesn't have to be another person standing opposite you on the basketball court. It might be that tough piece of music you're trying to play, or a history test you want to ace, or even the part of you that is afraid to fail. Does anyone win all the time? No. There will be times when you lose, but you still must say, to beat me you'll have to give it your all, because I sure am giving it my best. To turn any NO into YES, you must be competitive and unafraid.

....

⊛ *Look at NO as a challenge, something to be overcome.*

....

If you're competitive you always have a chance, and that's what you want. There may be a NO staring you in the face, but if you can compete against it with drive, passion and determination, you have a real chance to turn it into a YES. When you're successful, you know you've earned it. But even when you fall short you should be proud of your effort. You've done all you could, worked hard and tried to find a way to come out on top. Either way there will be no need for excuses. You were able to compete and become stronger, and that's all you can ask.

If you don't feel competitive enough, then take a look at someone who is competitive. Watch what he does and try to emulate him. If you want better grades and to be near the top of your class, look at some of the other top students. If one or more are going to the library every weekend, then you go, too. By doing this you are not only competing, but setting high standards for yourself. There's an inner strength in everyone and you can show it quietly. There's no need for a lot of talking and bragging when you turn a NO into YES. You know you've done it, and that should be enough. You just move on to the next challenge and stay focused on your dream.

When I was young, I was a really fast runner. When I'd race, my coach would tell me to just compete against myself, not worry that I was leaving others behind. What he meant was no matter how easily I was winning races, I should try to do better each time out. And that's what you have to do when someone tells you NO. If you're competitive, you're a lot more likely not to accept a NO. Instead, you're ready to compete and you go out and press on until you've made the two letter word a three letter word—YES.

Knowing Your Limitations

There will be situations where no remains NO. Or, at the very least, a NO for the moment. Along the way, you may find that as hard as you try, you can't overcome a particular NO. It may be that your heart isn't in it or that you've lost your passion for it. If you're okay with that and your goal isn't that important to you, then it's all right if you stop trying. You have the right to just not turn a no into a yes anymore. The biggest disappointment comes when your heart is still in it and the passion is there, but you can't turn it into a YES.

My dad encouraged me to let my conscience be my guide. If you are passionate and can't turn something into a yes, maybe the time isn't right. You may not be physically or mentally ready for that particular thing, or you simply might have too much on your plate at the time and risk burnout if you continue. If that's the case, just put it aside. Time is on your side and—you can return and try again later.

How do you make the judgment in this kind of situation? You have to gauge how much passion you still have and what it still means to turn this NO into a YES. Do you wake up every morning thinking about it and saying to yourself, *this is what I want*? Sometimes you may just be too young to conquer a particular obstacle at that time. You may seek out advice and be told that you should wait two or three years, then try again. If you aren't sure, always ask questions. Not only should you ask what you have to do, but when is the best time to do it? Fail early, but succeed late. That's still winning and sometimes the smart way to do it.

Comparing

It's a natural thing to measure your abilities by comparing yourself to others. That's not a bad thing, but it's also important that you learn to compare yourself against yourself. In other words, as I've mentioned before, you have to try to compete against yourself. Try to challenge yourself and do better than you did the time before. The best measuring stick you have is yourself. That keeps you pretty much in control and makes it less likely that you'll be intimidated by others. If you sense you're getting better, that's the best growth chart you can have. You're moving forward and won't become discouraged.

If you see someone doing something that you want to do also, and then use that person to motivate you. Comparing in that way is good and can help you turn a NO into YES. You may want to be as good as someone else, but to get there you still have to do the work. To compare can be a good thing if it has a positive result. If it's negative, that is, if you feel you'll never be as good as the other person, then comparing has a discouraging effect. If you remain discouraged and don't do the work, then you're setting yourself up for failure. Then NO remains NO.

Right to left: Dawn, Lisa, Teresa, and Nikki

Ruthie Bolton. Teammates are excited for the 1996 Olympics

When I was with the National team for the first time, I wanted more playing time. To do that, I knew I needed to become a much better defensive player. I began watching Nikki McCray who received many accolades for her defense. Nikki was much younger than me and extremely talented. She was quick and explosive on the court. Instead of being jealous, I emulated her work ethic and technique. We became extremely competitive with each other (it got really physical at times). To this day, we remain the best of friends because of our mutual work ethic.

We made each other better. Other players I learned from were Teresa Edwards, Lisa Leslie, and Sheryl Swoopes. They were great leaders. They taught me how to be confident, just relax, and play the game. Another player that I must mention is Dawn Staley. She taught me about fighting and competitiveness. I took many big shots because she passed me the ball.

I realized I needed a lot of individual work. I needed to become much stronger. So I went after it with no fear. I began lifting weights and doing everything else I could. I vowed I would be ready when my time came. If you are going to compare yourself to great players, to those who have already done it, then you've got to be ready to do the work to reach their level. That's the key.

Let me tell you a story about myself that I think takes into account almost all the elements that are being discussed in this chapter. It may have been my biggest challenge for turning a NO into a YES. It happened in 1998, just after I had competed with the National team at the World Championships in Germany. In the final game, we were losing to the Russians by 8 points with time running out. I had been on the bench and actually asked one of the assistant coaches to put me back in. They did. In the next five minutes I hit two big three-point shots, had two steals and we won the championship. We were all elated. I had harnessed my passion and produced great results. And guess who passed me the ball? Dawn Staley.

We all left the next day and I returned to Sacramento, where I was still playing for the Monarchs. We had taken time off to play in the World Championships.

Ruthie and the USA All Decade Team

The Monarchs were playing their fifth game of the season in Detroit when the coach sent me in. I didn't realize how tired I was. My legs felt tight. I guess the adrenaline of winning the World Championship still had me on clouds. I must have been on the court about two minutes when I drove toward the hoop and then stopped to take a jump shot. I actually heard my left knee pop and fell back in excruciating pain. I knew from the sound and the pain that it was bad.

They flew me back to Sacramento for an MRI and the news wasn't good. Both the interior cruciate ligament and medial cruciate ligament were sprained and the anterior cruciate ligament was completely torn. It was a very serious injury and would require reconstructive surgery. The doctor who normally would have done the surgery was on vacation and I couldn't wait. Eric Heiden was the doctor who just joined the team and he wound up doing the surgery. In case you don't recognize the name, Dr. Heiden was a record setting speed skater who won five gold medals in the 1980 Olympic Games at Lake Placid, New York. But he gave up his skating career and tons of potential endorsements to become a doctor. That was his real passion.

The surgery wasn't easy. Besides the ligament damage there was a lot of torn cartilage. Dr. Heiden told my trainer that I would never be 100 percent or play at the same level again. After my trainer gave the news to me, I spoke to Dr. Heiden who said he hoped some of the cartilage would regenerate, but it couldn't be replaced. I was also 30 years old, no longer a young athlete. Dr. Heiden told me I could have a second surgery, but that one would take several years to fully heal.

So there it was. I wasn't ready to give up my basketball career yet but was being told NO by knowledgeable medical people. NO, you'll never play at the same level again. For an athlete, hearing news like this can be crushing. But I wasn't ready to quit, to just accept NO, You Can't. That wasn't me. I refused to listen and started working extra hard at my therapy. My attitude was that no one was going to tell me this was the end. Only I could tell myself that.

Right away there were naysayers. People were expecting me to announce my retirement and the local paper said I had made a bad decision to try to come back, that I was getting older and had a good career. One newspaper called me old and rusty. That also motivated me. I began on crutches, unable to put any weight on the leg. Finally, I could walk a bit and I began making a lot of progress. In fact, they said I was about a month ahead of schedule when I hit a plateau and then didn't improve for a while. My trainer said that was normal.

But I wanted results and began going to the gym for extra work in the evening. That upset my trainer who didn't want me to hurt myself. I just figured the harder I worked the faster I could get back on the court. Six months after the surgery, I felt I was ready. But I still couldn't play hard. I played a bit in the summer of 1999, but there was still no way I could play in a big game. It took about nine months for me to feel like my old self. I came back to make the WNBA All-Star Team and then another Olympic Team in 2000. I just had the will and the drive to prove the doctors and the statistics wrong. I had made what sounded like a definite NO become a resounding YES! I even helped our Olympic Team win another gold medal in 2000—my second Olympic gold medal. I beat the odds!

Ruthie with Dr. Eric Heiden

Ruthie hugging teammate Teresa after the 2000 Olympics in Australia

The knee was achy at times and I had a second minor surgery to clean it up a bit, but my recovery was complete. Dr. Heiden said he was both surprised and impressed with the way I came back. He told me he had heard about how hard I worked, but admitted he never imagined I'd come back so strong after the kind of surgery I had. "You fooled all of us," he said, adding he was thrilled by it. That meant so much to me since he was a former Olympian.

For me, it was the ultimate NO to YES story. Expert doctors and trainers had said no you can't. But, I still had that burning passion and something inside me that said I could do it. I never thought twice about working to defy the odds. But it was really me working against me. If I had to do certain kicking exercises and was told to do 25 one day, I'd want to do 30 the next day. I just didn't want to leave any room for a letdown.

I simply couldn't see my career ending with an injury. I'd never know whether I could come back if I didn't try. Some people said I had a different level of drive. It was true I always loved physical action. But, when you're hurt you can't do the same things. Tearing an ACL in the knee humbles you and breaks you down. It's one of the worst injuries a basketball player can have. Many don't come back from it. But I was determined and put my entire being into my recovery, my heart and soul. I was absolutely determined that my basketball career wouldn't end with the word NO. Because of my will, drive, passion and work ethic, it didn't. I worked through the pain and agony of defeat and found success again.

I didn't quit and I didn't fail. Attitude and mindset won out. I think that's something everyone can learn from.

The Overall Importance of Turning No Into Yes
NO is certainly an obstacle, something that can stop you in your tracks. People, however, tend to be creatures of habit. When you make it a habit of turning NO into YES, you develop a mindset, a bring-it-on, confident mindset. Once you've made it over other hurdles, you can make it over the next. It will become second nature to work extra hard and that carries over to other facets of life. By overcoming a NO you develop a habit that makes you stronger, less fearful, and it becomes part of your foundation.

Fear can choke a lot of people and keep them from achieving. When you go through life afraid, you not only don't trust a lot of people, you also don't trust yourself. When I see a kid playing sports and see that person isn't afraid of anything and has that proverbial ice water in his veins, you know that person has the stuff needed to turn NO into YES. It's a great feeling to have that, giving you a freedom to explore and try new things, as well as the ability to bounce back and persevere. People will be drawn to you and you'll be an inspiration to others.

If you don't quite turn a particular NO into YES, you'll still feel good because you know you gave 100 percent. Once you continue to do that you'll be even more successful at everything you undertake. I know people who tried very hard to make it in sports. They didn't have quite enough talent and came up short, but their effort made it possible for them to succeed in another field. There's always something else out there that will arouse your passion, and you will have the desire and drive to get to where you want to be. So by tackling every NO that comes you're way you'll put yourself in a win-win situation with the courage to always try, to step up to the plate, no matter what the odds.

By doing that you'll also teach other people. When you constantly turn a NO into YES there's a ripple effect. People learn from your actions, see your drive, and watch the way you don't give up. They learn not from what you say, but from your actions. In summing up, let's list the qualities a person needs to turn NO into YES.

1. A positive attitude
2. Confidence
3. Passion
4. Enthusiasm
5. Determination
6. Belief or faith
7. An optimistic attitude
8. A strong work ethic
9. Not getting discouraged easily
10. Not having a fear of failure

When Do You Accept NO?

In some ways, you have to learn to accept NO early, especially when told you can't do something by your parents. That also teaches you to accept authority and to respect your parents. So as a young child, you must accept no without question and hope that your parents won't say no when something is in your best interests. Your parents are looking out for you and they aren't the enemy. Other people may not have your best interests at heart.

Don't always feel you're a failure when you have to accept a no. There are just some things you can't do while you're young. As you get older you'll be making more of your own decisions. There will still be times when you must accept no, when you've given it all and lost your passion. If you no longer have the passion and will to pursue something, then it's time to look elsewhere. That particular thing just wasn't for you. Everyone can't succeed at everything. So you have to gauge your limitations. You may not have the physical ability to excel at a sport. You may not have enough natural talent to become a good singer or musician. You may excel at History and English, but not at Math and Science. That doesn't mean you shouldn't try hard, but you have to know when you've reached your limits.

Accepting no under certain circumstances may be the best thing you can do. If, for example, you don't have the talent to be a college basketball star despite working hard for several years, accept it. You can still enjoy the sport on a recreational or intramural level. So part of turning NO into YES is knowing your limitations and also knowing just where to focus your passion and drive. Once you have the confidence and will to succeed, you'll find the right niche, a place where nothing can stop you from being all you can be.

Ruthie Bolton wearing her Monarchs jersey that turned her NO into a YES

Basic Steps For Turning NO Into YES
While the formula might not be quite the same for everyone, here are the basic steps you should consider when looking to turn a NO into YES.

1. Know that this is something you want and that it is very important to you.
2. Decide what it will take to reach your objective. List the things you must do. For example, if you want to be a singer look into taking vocal lessons, listen to others and then enter competitions.
3. Ask questions. Reach out to those you trust and make a list of possible resources that can help.
4. Read the stories of other successful people. What did it take for them to make it?
5. Start doing it. Implement the first steps and continue from there.
6. Find people along the way to advise, guide and encourage you.
7. Don't worry if you plateau. Keep working and progress will begin again.

8. Don't be discouraged.
9. Set short terms goals at first. Take it step by step and you'll see the NO beginning to dissolve.
10. Keep your passion at a continuously high level.
11. Constantly reassess the situation. How far do you want to go to make it a YES? It is important to keep fighting.
12. Remember not to ignore your other obligations, whether it's at school or at home. Always balance your time.

Do all these things as you travel down the road of life and you'll find confidence and drive, discover a solid work ethic, and don't lose your fear of failure. You'll ultimately succeed at the things you want the most.

CHAPTER EIGHT
RISING TO CHALLENGES

Life is a continual series of challenges. That's just the way it is and always has been. Yet challenges, as well as adversities, bring out the best in us and make us stronger. They keep us on our toes. In a sense, challenges are part of the survivor mode, enabling us to use what God has given us. Let's face it: life would be boring and predictable if we didn't have constant challenges to face. They keep our tools sharp. They make us better people if we learn to deal with them well. Everyone should learn to embrace challenges for a number of important reasons. The experience can be extremely educational because it teaches us about ourselves and then prepares us for the next challenge, which is sure to follow.

To experience your own "Ride of a Lifetime," you must be prepared to overcome all types of challenges. In fact, there have been so many challenges in my own life that I now embrace them with confidence. There's a good reason for that. One way to learn how to embrace and rise to challenges is to learn from someone who has been there and done that.

One of My Biggest Challenges

A large portion of my life revolved around basketball. You already know about the challenge I had making the team at Auburn University followed by the National team and then the Olympics. My time in the WNBA was smoother, until I tore my ACL and had the challenge of coming back from that injury and going on to win my second Olympic gold medal. So when it came to basketball, I had many difficult challenges and through hard work and perseverance, rose to conquer them all. Even though I knew that all sports careers must come to an end, nothing fully prepared me for the challenge of giving up my career and then finding a second, more meaningful one.

If you recall, I wasn't really ready to retire, but circumstances and a coach who didn't know me well, forced it. I had mixed emotions during what became a bittersweet time. My jersey was retired by the Monarchs, which was a great honor. While I was grateful, I still had the feeling that something was incomplete despite my long and successful career. There was another reality. I knew I had to transition to something else, something new and different, and I wanted it to be meaningful. I was dealing with some anger and frustration, which is never a good thing. What I knew I had to do was learn from what had happened and grow. I needed to find a better place and that was the real challenge. I also knew I needed spiritual direction, so I prayed often. Soon, I began to feel that the negative emotions would pass, no matter how difficult leaving basketball was, and that I'd eventually get through it.

The next step was to assess the entire situation and evaluate my life to that point so I could hopefully find where I wanted it to go next. I realized again the importance of having true character, something my dad had always talked about. I had to draw upon my inner strength and from my dad's teachings to get through it. A negative attitude was trying to consume me. I had doubts. My dad always taught us to get away from dark places and that your attitude is all-important when dealing with anger and doubt.

It's hard when you feel mistreated and still don't know your next step. Sometimes that mountain looks so high you feel you can't climb it. When I first looked into the future, I didn't know if I could take on this challenge because it was such a difficult transition. But because I had learned how to deal with anger and to discipline myself as an athlete, I persevered through this difficult time. Many people only saw the glamour of my professional basketball career, two Olympic gold medals, and two world basketball championships. They thought I had it all. Most never knew how challenged I felt.

I had to take it slowly and just step away from everything for a bit. It was almost as if I was in a holding pattern. When we act quickly, our emotions can overtake us and cause us to behave immaturely. The waiting is the toughest part, but necessary to the whole process. Nothing good happens overnight. I just asked God to help me and looked for the strength provided day by day. I wanted to remove any anger and resentment from my mind. If I gave into anger and carried all that frustration and anger with me, I felt I would be cheated out of the joyful part of my life. When I made my decision, I knew I finally had a solid grip on things. I felt balanced and ready. Even as a Monarchs player, Ruthie became a great mentor to young people.

My decision was to transition my career into being a mentor and motivational speaker for young people, to teach them all the things I had learned. I wanted to help them with the myriad of problems they are facing in today's world. I felt that the teachings of my dad, as well as my own experience from childhood right to the present, had prepared me to undertake this new task, I knew this path wouldn't be easy.

Everything in life contributed to my rising to this challenge. Instead of being defeated, I turned this challenge into a victory. Through it all, I kept hearing my dad's voice and everything he had taught me. All lessons of life well learned. I was fortunate to have someone like him to give me the solid foundation that would help me make it through this challenge. It allowed me to grow and blossom to the point where I can now share my life lessons with young people.

That foundation is all-important when taking on challenges. In sports, you need a strong core to help you breathe better, recover more quickly and have more stamina. In life, your character is your core, your DNA, your lifeline. I was challenged a lot in life, beginning when I was very young. While that didn't make the big challenges less daunting, it gave me the confidence and the ammunition to get through and overcome. Using everything I learned, I can once again say...I made it! I enjoy speaking to young people all over the United States.

Challenges Begin Early

Everyone has challenges in life before they even realize it. Just learning to walk and talk as a baby is a challenge. Because babies don't know fear, they struggle to get up and walk, no matter how many times they fall down. They'll work to learn new words because they want to be able to communicate with their parents and siblings. If the light comes on at an early age and you begin to embrace all new challenges, you are already ahead of the game and stronger for it. That's when you should begin looking for challenges.

As a child, I looked for larger puddles and higher fences to jump, as well as bigger, stronger weeds to pull out when helping in the fields. Every day was a challenge to do something better than I had done the day before. I was determined to try new activities. There are people, however, who begin to fear challenges early. They will have an even harder time with the bigger challenges that come later because they haven't strengthened their core.

On many occasions, you don't even have to look for challenges when you're young. They will find you. There are challenges often lurking around the next corner, a series of mini-challenges every day when you're young. Behaving in school can be a challenge for a youngster who likes to talk. Getting a better grade on a test is another major challenge. After school, the challenge may be completing your chores or playing ball and competing with your friends. Maybe it's the dance or music lessons you are taking after school that challenges you. Take the challenges head on and seek constant improvement. This teaches you to always strive to do the best you can and to take on the next challenge with no fear and a positive mindset.

Having a good self-image and strong foundation are important tools to carry with you. If you don't get support at home try to find it elsewhere.

Sometimes you have to reach out for help and direction. If you find yourself beginning to shy away from challenges at an early age and feel you are floundering, then it's time to go seek advice and help. You will sometimes meet someone at just the right time. If you have a mindset to keep pushing, people will appear in your life to give you extra strength.

Another thing to do when you're young is to watch other people who rise to challenges—maybe a classmate or friend. The experience of others can serve as a great teaching tool, so ask questions. I used to love coming off the bench early in my basketball career because I felt I could learn by watching those on the court. I learned both from their successes and their mistakes. If there was a certain player who was very good on the other team, and I would watch the opponent's style of play. Then, when I got into the game, I was better prepared to beat them at their own game.

At any rate, don't hesitate to tell a successful person how impressed you were by what he or she accomplished. Then ask how they did it. Most people will help you. You'll sometimes meet someone who can teach and influence you at just the right time. Remember, it's never too late to find direction or ask for support. Sometimes I feel that God chooses when to put people in our life.

When you rise to challenges it's about your whole being, and your mindset. Some kids will find that good mindset early on, which means that they have acquired a solid foundation one way or another. A few just seem to have the wisdom they need naturally. Others just need a little push and some good advice. Some, however, must find a great deal of help as rising to challenges comes much more slowly. They, too, must take it one step at a time and keep moving forward.

Because there will always be new challenges awaiting you in life, don't avoid any opportunity to learn. It's also a good idea to read stories about those who have overcome difficult challenges. It's another chance to learn. You may not have the exact same challenge you're reading about, but the method they used can certainly help you with the challenges you will face. The bottom line: you can't be timid or shy. Use all your resources, and don't be afraid to ask questions. A question will usually get an answer. Many of these answers will help you more than you know.

To Create or Wait for Challenges

Then there's the question of whether you should create challenges or wait until they come to you. It really works both ways. Challenges will come to you in different forms. There are many you won't have to look for. Just embrace them when they find you. I've always felt there's a reason you're chosen to take on a particular challenge. These challenges will be different for each person. The thing everyone has in common is when a challenge arises, they must immediately look for ways to overcome it. If you decide there is something you want to strive to achieve, then you are creating your own set of challenges. Whenever you have a dream or a goal, there will be challenges waiting at every turn until you reach your ultimate destination. If you decide you want to play basketball on the collegiate level, but feel you won't make it, then you're quitting before you start. Everything you want that is good will have challenges waiting for you, both large and small.

What you can't do is fear the challenge and never attempt to overcome it. You'll feel so much better about yourself when you persevere and meet the challenge head on. But that's a decision only you can make. The challenges will be there and it's up to you to accept them and then persevere. There will always be a series of small challenges on the road to overcoming the larger one. When the coach at Auburn University told me my chances of playing were slim, I had to decide what to do. The small challenges were improving every aspect of my game, beginning by working to get stronger and quicker, then improving my ball-handling, passing, shooting and defense. Each was a small challenge that took me on the route to becoming a very good player. When you work hard, and sacrifice things along the way, then you've truly earned your reward. There's no better feeling in the world.

There certainly may be times when a challenge is just too big. You'll know it because you will not make enough progress, and also by the fact that you'll find yourself losing motivation and drive. It's very difficult to overcome challenges without drive. If you find, for instance, that you don't want to practice the piano any more, it could be the composition you're trying to play is too difficult for your skill level. Then, it might be time to step back and re-evaluate. If you continue without motivation and passion, it can drain you of energy instead of providing you with it.

Ask yourself key questions. Is this challenge important enough for me to continue? Do I love it enough? Do I have a real passion for it? How much does this mean to me in the long run? Sometimes you simply have to take a couple of steps back before moving forward again. With the piano, play songs or do exercises that are right for your skill level and keep playing them until you feel you have mastered those songs and it's time to move on once again. In other words, you're making the challenges smaller and tackling them in smaller steps. This is the way to go if a challenge seems overwhelming; you should continue to pursue it.

If you still love the challenge, chances are you'll find a way to get it done. Slow down or even put it aside for awhile. When you return to it you can better answer the above questions and then decide whether to return and pursue it with increased motivation and drive. I didn't make the 1992 Olympic team, simply because I didn't have enough skills at the time, though I gave it my all when I tried. I stepped back, analyzed my strengths and weaknesses, and then began working harder. When the next Olympic team was chosen four years later, I was more than ready. It took four years, to overcome that challenge, but I never lost my passion for the game.

You really have to learn to assess a challenge and determine whether you are ready or not. Sometimes it's simply a matter of maturing physically or mentally, before taking on a larger challenge. As part of assessing a particular challenge, it's always good to seek advice from someone in that field or even one who has overcome a similar challenge. You may find a person who will tell you that you can do it. That's what happened with me when I didn't receive an invitation to try out for the Olympic Team in 1992. Carol Ross, who was an assistant coach at Auburn University, believed in me and told me that I could do it. She helped me find the confidence and gave me that extra push that led me to pay my own way to the Olympic trials a few years later. I was ecstatic to win a spot on the 1996 Olympic team!

What about different types of challenges? There are many, some small, others larger and some that continue for most or all of your life. The challenges to be a better person are almost everywhere. Just dealing with friends at school and being accepted by other kids is a challenge. Dealing with a death in the family or parents divorcing is a major challenge. Your family moving to another city also presents a challenge since you have to adjust to new surroundings, a new school and making new friends. You must develop confidence deep in your soul so that you can overcome these challenges. Look for the gold within yourself. Connect to your inner winner wherever you may be.

Take the challenges on and seek constant improvement.

Functioning well within the family unit can also be challenging. It's a challenge to be a good brother or sister and a better son or daughter. You never stop developing as you grow. Maybe you can help around the house more. All of these things become a series of challenges and part of your total being and character. As you grow, you'll be dealing with hormonal changes, then with boyfriends and girlfriends. To keep moving forward and avoid being detoured by bad decisions is a huge challenge in your formative years.

Part of the key, is to keep a balance and keep an empowering company. Kids today, often spend too much time on the computer, the cell phone, in front of the television, and not doing homework. If you aren't doing well in school, the challenge is to find that balance and resist the temptations of today's enhanced communication devices. There's no substitute for good, old-fashioned work and dedicated study time. That's what it takes to do well in school. Be disciplined with your time, be honest with your parents, and do the right things with friends that empower and uplift you and your spirits.

USA All Decade Team after winning the Olympics

I've heard many kids today say they are overwhelmed by school, and sometimes they resist the people who are trying to guide them. I tell these kids that they are bound to make mistakes. Then I challenge their mindset. Most parents know the importance of structure and discipline, so listen to them. You may, for instance, know the foods you are eating are unhealthy. Even if you like them, make a change for the better. Learn to do the right thing in all areas of your life. The challenge is to be a better person with each passing day. This isn't easy. Life is full of temptations, so making the right choices and decisions is important.

Another important ingredient in rising to all the aforementioned challenges is confidence. Confidence gives you the drive to move forward. It also gives you more zest and enthusiasm. Many kids today lack that kind of confidence and this can hurt them. I know a girl who can sing very well but lacked the confidence to sing in public. I finally convinced her to sing for other people and she became more confident each time she performed. Finally, she sang at a talent show. I would tell her that the more she did it, the better she would become. I also advised her that she's singing for a reason and should have fun if she loved it that much.

There are times, when you will also begin to lose confidence if you don't overcome a particular challenge. I can remember it happening to me during a basketball game. I would suddenly lose my shot or fail to make some key free throws. When you begin thinking too much, you choke your natural rhythm. It feels like a snowball rolling down a hill. That's when you must step back and return to the basics. It's always a good idea when you begin losing confidence to go back to the drawing board and draw from your strength. Go back to the things you were doing when it was all happening for you. In other words, think about how it was when you had the confidence. Evaluate everything mentally and refocus on the task before you. Don't become complacent, angry or frustrated. Keep focusing on the positive and begin doing the small things once again that contributed to your success.

Confidence is extremely important. It increases your adrenaline and is part of your mojo. If you allow too much time to pass without stepping back to assess your progress, you'll be in even more of a slump. Then, it will be more difficult to get that confidence back. Sometimes more practice and working harder helps, such as when you're trying to get your shot back in basketball. But you can also back away from the thing that is not working and return to something you know you are good at. That's yet another way to get your confidence to return. Do something smaller and maybe not quite as important to you now, but things that gave you confidence in the first place. If you were confident about yourself and your challenges before, you can get there again.

The Dynamics of Fear

There are all kinds of fears and they can be crippling to someone who wants to rise to a big challenge. There is physical fear, the fear of failure, the fear of ultimately not being successful, the fear of people making fun of you and the fear of looking foolish. These are all fears that come into place when you are trying to rise to a challenge. When you begin your pursuit you have to understand you will make mistakes. You can't worry about what other people may think; nor can you be perfect right away. Exhale, release the fear and focus on your strengths.

I can remember when I was in the military in 1987, the training in ROTC was very difficult. Most of the work out was very challenging. They do this for several reasons: 1) to get you in shape and increase your physical skills, and 2) to help you conquer your fears. They break down each task, telling you exactly how to do it. I was afraid of heights, but I had to climb a wall and then repel down the other side. The instructors talked about the necessary safety measures constantly until you knew them all effectively. They went over all the rules again and again. They emphasized that people don't get hurt if they followed the safety measures the right way. My 10 year military service helped me to conquer my fear of heights and fear of falling. I finally did it!

Another way to lose fear is to build confidence. If a young athlete is afraid to wrestle because he thinks he will lose, then he has to bolster his confidence by building strength. He should run to increase his endurance, do pushups, and maybe some supervised weight training. Once he feels himself becoming stronger, he'll also become more confident. I used to fear having to take the last-second free throw that would mean winning or losing the game. I also knew that good players want to be in that position and I wanted to be a good player. So I began preparing by imagining that situation in practice, then taking the free throw. I did that repeatedly and it gradually prepared me for doing it in a game. By working harder and visualizing the situation, I overcame my fear and made a lot of big game shots.

If you fear failing because others will make fun of you, then you have to change your mindset. You have to understand who you are and what is important to you in life. To that end, you can't let the words of others bother you. Keep telling yourself that you are important and special, and that you won't be intimidated by others. Rise above your fears.

Anytime you try to overcome a difficult challenge, you will make some mistakes and experience some failure. You need to develop a mindset that won't allow anything to keep you from achieving your goal and overcoming the challenge. Don't allow other people to get into your head with negative thoughts that lead to fears. Remember, it isn't how many times you get knocked down, but the number of times you get back up.

Life as a Series of Challenges

As a kid I was quiet, but not afraid of anything. In that sense, I was being prepared and conditioned to face challenges. The more I overcame the more confidence I had. It reached a point where I felt I could do anything. But as you know, there were some huge challenges ahead of me and, like everyone else, I had some doubts and needed help. But that solid foundation from my dad and the fact that I faced a series of small challenges early on, helped me to regroup and continue when things got rough. You must embrace challenges because they teach you a great deal about yourself. I think it's a real gift to learn how to persevere and overcome. There are motivational speakers earning huge fees for teaching people how to do things such as overcoming challenges. You can do this too on a smaller scale. Once you begin to overcome small challenges, don't hesitate to help friends and classmates who may have problems with similar challenges. By doing that, you're helping yourself as well.

🏵 *It isn't how many times you get knocked down, but the number of times you get back up.*

The Challenge of an Abusive Marriage

This is something I don't talk about very often, but I was in an abusive marriage for a substantial period of time. I learned all over again that no one is exempt from troubles and struggles. It was really difficult from about 1993 to 1997. During that period I made the Olympic team and we won the gold medal. That's where I excelled, and felt free. It helped me get through an otherwise difficult period. I endured both mental and physical abuse, but stayed in the marriage another five years, probably because I've never been a quitter and thought I could fix it.

Finally, I made the decision to leave. I came through this difficult period with the right mindset. I feel I learned from it and harbor no resentment. Because I did not allow this challenge to consume me or interfere with my career, I consider it a victory. It was a part of my development and helped make the next challenge less daunting.

In a sense, you can look at life as an obstacle course. It becomes more difficult as you move along, but all challenges prepare your body and mind for what lies ahead. You'll improve your stamina and your life experience. Stick it out and triumph. Afterwards, you will have a story to share with your siblings, friends, daughter, son, nieces and nephews—all kinds of people. You just might be the one who helps someone else make it through the tough spots in life. Your advice and experience might keep someone from doing drugs or thinking about ending their life. Yes, it can be that extreme for some.

People are inspired by other people. Your struggles will help others once they know about how you have dealt with challenges and the hard times they sometimes bring. The stamina you will build by rising to challenges will make you an interesting and inspiring person. Goals and dreams will all become challenges, and some will create adversity that must be overcome. You have to appreciate the value of your struggles. They are lessons that free your mind and soul for greater accomplishments. Others will see just how you overcame them and the positive mindset you have developed along the way.

Yes, life is a series of challenges. That's part of the journey and part of the ride. Getting to those difficult destinations is all part of being successful. Look at it as a long drive. There are going to be roadblocks—rain, snow and construction—things which will slow you down. There will be times when you have to take a detour, but when you are once again riding on that straight open road, you'll appreciate it all the more. Knowing you could have quit and gone home but didn't, will give you a certain kind of grace. You'll see the value in what you're trying to achieve and realize that it is all worth it. Going through challenges and surviving them is crucial. Thriving in the midst of a challenge is so vital to your whole being, your soul and your spirit.

Don't ever quit, because you are now beginning your ride of a lifetime!

Steps to Overcoming Challenges

Just to summarize, I'm going to list the basic steps needed to rise to and overcome challenges. The information presented in the chapter could serve as a template for what you need as a person and how to put your skills together with a positive mindset to overcome nearly anything, especially those things you really want. Let's take a look.

1. Know just what the challenge is. Assess it fully. Decide if it's important enough to overcome and ask yourself if you are ready to overcome it. That means checking your passion and enthusiasm levels.
2. Figure out exactly what you have to do to overcome the challenge. Put together an action plan about how are you going to get there.
3. Ask yourself if you are willing to make the necessary sacrifices.
4. Know that the solution won't happen overnight and you might plateau at some point. As long as you keep your passion and enthusiasm, you'll keep moving forward.
5. Always seek help, advice and encouragement from others when you need it.
6. Don't be discouraged if your progress isn't as fast as you hoped.
7. If necessary, take small steps instead of larger ones. Make it a series of smaller challenges.
8. Never forget how good you will feel when you reach your goal and realize you have overcome a major challenge.

I really learned how to appreciate the value of our struggles and overcoming challenges while training young women in Saudi Arabia to play basketball. I was part of the Jetta United Saudi Arabia organization working with the U.S. Embassy to empower Saudi Arabian girls. I admired their commitment and dedication to basketball. Most importantly, I admired how these young women handled the challenge of only having at most two hours during their day to play a sport and be totally unencumbered by their required traditional dress that covered nearly every inch of their bodies when they were in public. They maximized the moment and their freedom from restrictions when they played ball with us. They reminded me to appreciate my freedom to play and to dress without restrictions or boundaries. Their passion touched my heart. I wished I could spend more time with them. Experiences like this motivated me even more to share my story.

Remember, once you have risen to meet a challenge, the next one won't seem so difficult. You're on your way to becoming the person you want to be, with confidence and without fear!

CHAPTER NINE
WINNING AT LIFE

Winning at life is the ultimate challenge, the goal and quintessential dream. The reason is simple. Everyone has a right to have a great life. Each individual has a unique fingerprint from birth, and has a right to craft a unique life experience. It's never too late to be the person you want to be. Express yourself and have the courage to stand up for yourself. In a free society you always have choices. When you make the right choices, you can have a great life.

Make the choices that help fulfill your dreams. Ask yourself, how can I be better today than I was yesterday? Am I learning and becoming wiser each day? Do I keep getting closer to what I really want from life? These are questions to ask yourself as you grow and mature. When you ask these questions daily, you have the opportunity to make adjustments that will place you closer to your ultimate dream.

Winning at life means you are passionately pursuing your goals. At the end of the day, look in the mirror and be happy with what you see. Treating others well is also part of the equation. It's not necessary to make a pile of money to win at life. There are people who are struggling financially and have beautiful relationships and beautiful families all working together. Winning at life is an ongoing pursuit of happiness. Look at it this way. If life is a song, sing it. If life is a game, then play it. If life is a struggle, overcome it.

The majority of people I speak to are young girls and my main message is to try to help them get the foundation needed to become all they can be. There is an organization called Playmakers that helps boys become men who go on to become great husbands and great fathers. Their objective is to build character. Character and foundation building are important. They enable young people to achieve and seek happiness and gain joy from their lives while reaching for the stars.

We all continue to evolve during our lifetime as we deal with change. Detours are all part of life. You simply learn how to stay the course. Winning at life is a long journey and something you continually work at. That's why a good foundation is so important. It does not matter what car you drive or what house you live in. Home is a place where you can be happy and content. Michael Jackson was worth millions of dollars, yet despite his many successes, it saddens me to know there was still something keeping him from enjoying his life. Remember, money isn't the answer to everything.

USA All Decade Team on the court after winning the 2000 Olympics in Australia

Start When You're Young

If you go to college, the first two years are to build a foundation towards your major. If you play a sport, build a strong foundation by strengthening your body. Develop a strong core and increase your stamina. My program is all about giving kids the basic essentials to succeed in life. It's about attitude, integrity, accountability, controlling anger and overcoming challenges. You must have all these qualities no matter what you ultimately pursue as your life's work. Adapting to these qualities early gives you the stamina and ability to stay with your pursuits. When you draw from your foundation, it's easier to overcome challenges and rebound from setbacks. You jump over life's hurdles more smoothly and bounce up faster if you fall. Your foundation is essential; it makes you stronger in every way.

Create good habits and routines that strengthen your foundation. Changing bad habits early on will propel you forward. It is never too late to change a bad habit. You *can* teach an old dog new tricks, if he is willing to change.

Most kids want success and want to win at life, but sometimes there are things holding them back. A lack of confidence or self-esteem, fear of rejection, fear of letting people down, and negative peer pressure may keep you from reaching your goals. If you want to be successful, be willing to do the work needed to overcome all obstacles. You must have a winning attitude and surround yourself with positive people who lift you up and give you energy. Negativity sucks the life out of you.

Positive people make you feel good about yourself. They encourage you to do the right thing. You might not realize it early on, but eventually you will recognize people who are on your side. These are the people you need to have around you, even if it is someone you can only call or text. That's what I did with my dad. He was always very positive and uplifting. Now I have friends like that who are on my side, looking out for my best interests and I feel good talking to them. Never be hesitant to approach positive people. Talk to them, ask questions and spend time with them, even if they aren't a friend. Tell them you: 1) like what they're about, 2) have good vibes about them, and 3) ask them to be a friend. It works.

Kids who are moving in the wrong direction have to know that it's never too late to make improvements. They have to reach out for help and direction, understand they are not perfect, and be willing to learn from their mistakes. There are always people out there who care for and love you, whether it's parents, relatives, teachers, coaches or clergymen. At the same time, you need to break away from the wrong kinds of friends. Seek people who are moving in the direction that you want to go, and don't let peer pressure get to you.

Doubting yourself at times is a natural thing. Everyone has doubts. One way to remove doubt when undertaking a particular task is to gather information. Do your research and get information from people who have experience. These are small steps to build confidence and will carry over to other areas of your life.

....

🏵 *Winning at life is a long journey.*

....

Public Speaking

I had a fear of public speaking. I was terrified if I knew I had to speak in front of a group. I couldn't sleep the night before a speaking engagement. I sought advice from an expert, someone who was a really good public speaker. Then I began practicing and I got better by simply learning from my mistakes. It happened one step at a time. Speaking to groups is now a big part of my life, and to win, I simply had to overcome my public speaking fear. Now after hours of practice, I can honestly say my fear is gone.

Finding Your Best Qualities

To win at life you can't live with resentment and anger. You shouldn't even resent the setbacks or challenges you'll have along the way. These help you learn more about yourself. To win at life, you must understand what life is about. Setbacks humble you and perfect your character. When you deal with them, you can develop grace, a new perspective on life, and touch other people's lives. It isn't easy to reach the point of winning, yet once you teach people how to maintain and thrive in spite of their situation, you become very empowering.

Find new qualities inside of you. The tougher life is, the deeper you'll have to dig inside yourself and discover qualities you didn't know you had. Keep moving even if the unknown is directly in front of you. Once you make it through, the next time you encounter a roadblock it won't be so frightening. Remember these tips: 1) Take life by the horns; do not allow it to dictate to you; 2) Some challenges need a rapid response but, think before you react; 3) You will know when you are ready to fight a battle; whenever battles come, remember to be strong and confident; 4) Don't be ambushed by circumstances.

When I speak with groups of kids, most of them know what I've accomplished in basketball and that's how they look at me. But I want them to see beyond that and get to know the real me. If kids see you as a celebrity of any kind, they tend to put you on a pedestal. I don't want that. I want them to know I'm someone who really cares, that I'm a genuine person who is there for one reason only: I want to help them succeed. Part of my platform is that I was a basketball star, but I also want to be someone who makes an impact on their lives. That's why I tell them that I was once where they are and that I have been blessed to have done the things I've done. Hard work is what has helped me win at life. Nothing was handed to me. I described the ways I persevered and turned many NO's into YES's. I encourage you to do the same. I use the respect I receive as a celebrity to influence the kids I speak with, not as a way to brag about myself. I share my story with children in hopes that it will motivate them to develop their own passion and create the life they want for themselves. If it could happen to me, a small town girl from Mississippi with limited income and a family of 20 siblings, it could happen to them.

I can only hope that my story motivates others. I've reached many of my goals and dreams, and have overcome much along the way. In that sense, I've been a winner at life just for my efforts to achieve. Life rewards those who overcome challenges. That's what I emphasize; winning at life is within anyone's reach.

More on Character

To win at life, you must keep working on your character. Character is what keeps you grounded. It also gives you boundaries. Character goes hand in hand with ethics and integrity. Both ensure that you continue to do the right thing, even when no one is looking. Developing a character, is an important investment you make in yourself.

It's all a building process. In the beginning, you might not know just who you are and what you have inside. But every day you discover more about yourself. People who believe in you will help you find what you have inside. I don't know if I would have even gone to Auburn University had it not been for my dad and the way he believed in me. It was as if he saw inside me before I recognized what I wanted to do myself. He knew the value of hard work and felt I could make it. He always told me: It's what's inside that really counts.

Everyone reaches a point where they ask themselves, can I really do this? Take on the small challenges first. Even after you're successful with smaller things, a big obstacle, goal or challenge might still seem daunting. That's when you need some help and should tap into your support system.

Ruthie Bolton with Britney Shine and other future WNBA stars

Ben's Story

This may well be one of the ultimate stories of winning at life. It's a story about how a person overcame seemingly insurmountable challenges. Ben Underwood lost both his eyes to retinal cancer at the age of three. Yet he lived life to the fullest. Years later, I heard about this amazing young man. My friend and photographer, Felicia Rule really wanted me to meet him. He was from Sacramento, California. We met when I was speaking to an organization called Pride Industries for People with Disabilities. Ben was there with his mom and told me he wanted to meet me. From that day forward, our spirits connected.

Despite the loss of his vision, he never wasted a minute of his life. He was never sad and maintained a positive, upbeat attitude all the time. His enthusiasm for life was inspiring. He loved to sing, so we would sing every chance we got. He refused to allow his situation to get the best of him. He taught people to appreciate life and their vision. Despite his handicap, he had a total zest for life and a great presence. He was a winner at life.

Ben walked to school by himself. He could simply whistle and tell if there was something in front of him, a rare sense only some blind people develop. He could skateboard and ride a bike because of his amazing sense of awareness similar to sonar. People thought his mom was putting him in danger by allowing him to do these things, but she had confidence in his abilities. Ben did not complain. He made things happen for himself and learned how to adjust and adapt to change.

He went to a regular school and was a very good student. His plans for the future included attending college and having a singing career. His voice impressed Stevie Wonder so much he attended one of Ben's birthday parties. Ben was always optimistic. He never worried about the possibility of his cancer returning. He lived for every moment. One of the things he said was, "If I complain about something it won't change it. Nothing will bring my eyesight back."

Ben also had a great sense of humor. He made people around him laugh and was full of joy. His boundaries were limited, but that didn't stop him from aiming high. He had a great character and a solid foundation, and they served him well. Though Ben died at the age of 16, I'll never forget him. He had such a great attitude and confident mindset that it allowed him to be a winner at life. His story should serve as an inspiration to everyone who hears it, as it was for all those who met and knew him.

My Sister Betty

There are times when you don't have to look very far to find someone who is a winner at life. I didn't have to look any further than my older sister, Betty. She was the fourth oldest of the 20 children and now has ten children of her own. She married when she was 16 years old had to endure the tragedy of her husband's untimely death. She then raised the seven children alone. She struggled financially, barely making it. Dad used to tell her that no matter how bad it seemed, it wouldn't always be that way. He helped her, the same way he always helped me, and Betty was always joyful. You wouldn't know the kind of struggle she experienced. Betty remarried and had three more children. But her second husband also died. Even though both husbands died young, Betty held the family together and was an outstanding mother. Even though she missed much of her own childhood and regrets some of those early decisions, Betty still feels extremely blessed to have her 10 children.

Betty decided to become a teacher. She got her associate's degree and, believe it or not, was my kindergarten teacher. She returned to school and earned her B.A. degree and teaching credential. Some years later, she became certified to run a daycare center and reached yet another goal, opening Betty's Babies. Now, at age 58, with all her children grown and a grandmother many times over, Betty is going into her second year of operating her daycare center. She owns the business, which is located in Hattiesburg, Mississippi. She now has people working for her. She's so happy that she stuck with it and pursued her dream.

I admired Betty and her positive attitude. Never once did I see a misery-loves-company attitude about her. She also believed our dad when he said, "No matter how low you feel, you have to believe that this day will pass."

After becoming a successful teacher, Betty had to learn how to run a daycare center business. Betty's children banded together to form a gospel singing group called The Street Family (their name) that often performed locally. One of her sons is pursuing his musical talent and tried out for American Idol, making it all the way to Hollywood before falling short of the final group that went on the show. Another one of her sons attended college at Southern Mississippi University and continues to hold hope for making it to the NFL. Another daughter completed law school and is now a practicing attorney.

Betty was committed to making things work. She persevered. She remained positive and never made any excuses. "*This is what I have to do,*" she would say. "*This is my journey.*" And she kept moving forward. As with me, the things my dad said were what kept her going. We shared that great foundation he gave to us. Her kids all saw her strength and that has made them want to achieve on their own.

Betty is a winner at life. She used her positive attitude and strong character to create the rewarding life she deserved.

Aiming High

The Aim High program I now bring to schools and to groups of children is something that evolved after my basketball career ended. The idea first came from my experience in life and then, my experience transitioning from professional athlete to a life after basketball. My basketball career did not end as well as I would have liked. Despite the many things I had accomplished, I wasn't able to get the kind of closure I wanted.

There was confusion, disappointment and sadness surrounding my departure from the game. In a sense, I felt betrayed because I had given so much to the game. I began wondering, "*Why am I in this place?*" I knew I had to do some real soul searching. Dad was gone by then and he was the one I always turned to in times of trouble. I needed answers and turned to prayer and meditation. I reflected on my entire life, my career, and upon those things within myself I always drew from. People tried to help, but I really needed some solid direction.

This wasn't an easy time for me. I was angry and didn't want to retire. Nevertheless, I knew I had to work through it, and discipline myself to deal with other people's opinions. It took me a while to accept the fact I wouldn't be playing anymore. It was a very tough time. A few weeks later, I attended a Monarchs game and when I entered, I received an amazing standing ovation. There must have been seven or eight thousand people chanting, "RUTHIE! RUTHIE! RUTHIE!" and it blew me away. They literally stopped the game. They brought me to the center court and I told the fans I may not be on the court anymore, but I'm still committed to the game. I thanked them for their loving support. This gave me closure and I finally felt at peace.

🌀 *Never Give Up. Be a Winner at Life.*

I knew I had made the right decision to retire. Three weeks later, I accepted a position with the Monarchs' front office. The cheers and feelings of love I felt from the fans that night when I entered the arena convinced me to remain with the team. Up to that point, I had thought about leaving the team completely.

Soon after, it hit me. I really began to feel compelled to tell my story, to speak with groups of children and go into the schools. I wrote a program designed to show kids the importance of character. Then, I added integrity and attitude, all of which make up the center of my life force. All of these qualities are part of my foundation and have allowed me to aim high in life. AIM stands for Attitude in Motion, and my program emphasizes reaching for something higher than yourself. If you aim high, you won't always make the shot. But if you keep aiming high, the ball will ultimately bounce your way.

Remember, when you start to acquire these qualities as a young person you're investing in something that will produce a huge return someday. Keep doing the right thing no matter how difficult it may seem at times. You shoot for goals in life. You take aim at objectives. You move in a direction. But, if you don't care about shooting the ball, you won't even pick it up. My advice is to pick it up and see just how high you can go with it so you can make one winning shot after another until you reach the place you really want to be in your life.

Steps to Winning at Life
There are no hard and fast rules for winning at life. However, there are concepts and principles, things that will help get you there. Combine them with character and a positive attitude, and you've got that all-important chance to win.

1. Have a winning attitude, even when you don't always win.

Just come to play and believe you can win every time.

2. Set goals and be disciplined. Set both short and long-term goals.

3. Learn from others and learn from your mistakes. Don't be hesitant to reach out and ask for help. Use all your resources and do whatever is necessary to get the job done.

4. Have enthusiasm. It gives you a positive mentality, a deep joy and a sense of accomplishment. It allows you to embrace new things and endure whenever necessary.

5. Learn how to thrive and fight through things. Just keep pushing, push to the end, and don't take NO for an answer.

6. NEVER GIVE UP. Hang in there, even if you're hanging on by a thread. If you don't quit you will prevail.

7. Always strive for more, even after reaching a goal. Don't ever be completely satisfied, because there's always something else just around the corner.

8. Keep having fun. Enjoy what you're doing, relax and you'll enjoy the rewards even more.

9. Follow #1-8 and you'll BE A WINNER AT LIFE!

CHAPTER TEN
CONTINUING THE RIDE OF A LIFETIME

Remember, your "Ride of a Lifetime" will always continue. I know it will for me, and I'm wishing you the best. I can already envision the rest of my life. It will consist of community involvement, mentoring and developing youth, whether through coaching or my after school programs. That's my passion now, the thing that gets me excited. When I wake up each day I know that's my purpose in life and that is a good feeling to have.

Someday I would like to have a facility with a sign on the door that reads: YOU CAN ONLY COME IN HERE IF YOU VOW TO LEAVE AS A BETTER PERSON! I want to create an environment where youngsters can grow, study, work out, play sports and improve themselves. When I speak to groups, I want to have an impact on the lives of every person in the audience. So I also see myself traveling and continuing as a motivational speaker. Whenever I meet people, I always tell them about my vision.

I want to share my stories with girls and boys, and young women. My goal is to uplift and encourage them. This is my place I've found in the world. It is my purpose, and it's all a result of the things that happened in my past. Everything came together to help me choose this path. I know with absolute certainty that this is where I belong. I enjoy traveling, meeting and empowering people. I didn't fully understand my purpose until I tore my ACL, lost both my basketball career and my dad in a short period of time. Once I realized my real purpose in life, I was completely at peace. People always look for the best way to be effective. I know mine is trying to be a positive influence on young people.

What Could Have Happened

I often think what might have happened to me, and also to my siblings, had it not been for the excellent foundation and teachings of my dad. Without that foundation, we simply would not have made it. My dad encouraged me to embrace both fears and challenges. Without the foundation he gave me, I probably wouldn't have gone to Auburn University.

I was intimidated and frightened by the situation, but he was my leaning post. He gave me the confidence I needed to take that bus that changed my life, and ride it to the destination that started my basketball career. He also taught me about responsibility and to follow the rules. If you can't play by the rules, you just can't play.

In a nutshell, Dad's teachings put us in a position to excel. The things he taught us were more important than a bank account with a million dollars in it. Without his guidance and the foundation he gave us we could have been 20 brothers and sisters who just went through the motions and wound up staying home and probably working menial jobs. He urged us to choose something in life and then strive for it, to pursue excellence even if you fall short. My dad simply gave all of us the mentality to be the best we could be. He taught us not to settle for less. He also taught us to be happy and to seek peace. Otherwise, you won't have a good quality of life.

Without that foundation there's no telling where I would have ended up. I would have lacked confidence and had a fear of failure. I don't think it's too much of a stretch to say I could still be in McLain with few prospects for the future. Coming from a tiny town like that and without a foundation, I never would have gone out in the world. Sometimes you just don't see beyond the trees and there's no way to make it big from a small town until you have certain qualities. People living in the small town like McLain sometimes think you're crazy to dream that big. What I did is a testament to the teachings of my dad.

As I've said before, a strong foundation is your core. It gives you the stamina to bounce back. Your character, faith and attitude are your cornerstones. No matter what you want to do in life—nurse, doctor, athlete, astronaut or CEO of a company, that foundation will shape you and help you work through adversity. It contains your building blocks and your resource center, and you branch out from there.

My advice regarding a strong foundation will never change. If you aren't getting it at home, you must try to find it elsewhere. It's just a reality that some children don't come from a loving home. They have to reach out to a relative, teacher, coach, clergyman—someone they trust and admire, and who cares about people. Take the lead character in the movie, *The Blind Side*. He drew from the family that took him in. They gave him the building blocks he couldn't get from his own family. It is out there. You just have to seek it. There are many good Samaritans in the world. It's up to you to find one because you owe it to yourself.

 *The greatest risk to success is to take no risk at all.*

Giving Back

Now my life is about giving back, making a bigger impact off the basketball court than I did on the court. That's why community is so important to me. As much as I enjoyed playing, I'm just as hungry to try changing some young person's life as I was to hit the winning shot. This is actually more important because I'm trying to make a difference in young people's lives. Among other things, I try to get parents involved and impress upon them that we are a team and must work together. If we work as a team, it gives kids confidence. The chance to not only help kids through, but to also give parents guidance is a beautiful thing.

Part of continuing my ride of a lifetime is to be able to give strength to people, something that will help them through adversity and hard times. That's one of the greatest gifts I can receive. It's extremely satisfying to just be there for someone and give them a listening ear. So, all in all, it's a beautiful thing to be able to give. That's the part of my life now that I enjoy the most, giving and teaching kids to have a good attitude and not give up.

When I share my story with kids, it empowers me and hopefully does the same to those who are listening. I want my audience to see exactly who I am, a whole person and not just a basketball star who won gold medals and championships. That's secondary. I want them to see the valleys I went through and all the difficult times I overcame. I want them to know that my life was not always glory and excitement. Nobody's is like that all the time. That's why I want them to see ways in which they can overcome. I feel now that I'm obligated to share. I hope those who listen become better people through my story.

I once received a letter from a young girl who was part of an audience I was speaking to. What made it unusual is that she wrote the letter while I was speaking and presented it to me before I left. Her letter thanked me and said I had helped her see a number of things she hadn't been doing right and what she could do to improve herself. To get the feeling that I may have changed that person's life instantly felt even better than hitting a winning shot. It meant I was making a difference.

There is no limit to what I'm doing now. A sports career is always limited. It has to end sometime, even for the best of us. What I'm doing now will last a lifetime. I like to think that if all people ever remembered about me was that I was a great basketball player, then I must have done a bad job with the rest of my life. Fortunately, I've found a true purpose in my life. I feel I've become a person of even deeper confidence and an inspirational speaker because I have a story to tell and can do it with passion and sincerity. There's a spiritual drive within me and, in one way, my work now keeps my dad alive for me because I always share his teachings and the things he said. People are constantly telling me they wish they could have met him. That always makes me feel good.

Becoming a parent has opened my eyes even more and taught me things that winning two gold medals never could. Hope, my daughter, is now two and a half years old, while my son, Christofer Daniel Linwood Bolton, is three months old at this writing. I think by now it should be apparent that I've always loved kids, but there is nothing like having your own because they immediately become part of your existence. It's my responsibility to help shape them every day of my life. Dad always said that God blessed us with children. From their birth to when they are grown, we are responsible for shaping, trusting, and giving them wisdom. When they have reached a certain age in their life, we must let them make their own decisions and learn from their mistakes.

Ruthie holds 3-month old son Christopher, 2011

So this is the beginning of a new and rewarding journey for me. When you have children, your priorities must change and you have to plan life accordingly. In one sense, it defines the true meaning of life. A baby just wants you and unconditional love. They depend upon you completely. Young children appreciate the simple things. They teach us how to be free and how to keep life simple, and my children are now an integral part of my lifetime ride.

People who are not good parents can do irreparable damage to a child. I've seen much of it in my travels and my presentations to various groups of children. Many parents try but I know it can be difficult today for parents to teach children as my parents taught us. That's why I feel so compelled to speak with as many kids as possible. Many kids just need someone to listen to and encourage them. They may talk with the wrong person about their troubles and then find themselves in even more trouble.

There are some parents who have very busy lives and tend to ignore their children. That busy lifestyle, which may include trying to put food on the table, sometimes leads to parents not getting to really know their children. They are too busy paying attention to their kids' self-esteem, or lack of it. Children in this situation are missing one-on-one contact with a mentor and leadership from a parent or parents that they really need. They lack attention, but want to be heard. They also want to feel they belong to a loving, caring family.

I have a nephew who is in prison now. For some reason, he felt a need to belong to a gang. They were the wrong people. Sure enough, he got into trouble. It's an old story. A kid wants to feel important, wants to belong, and then he helps his "family" rob a store on the weekend. That's why peer pressure can be so difficult when it is primarily negative.

When we grew up, the most trouble we got into at school was for talking or chewing gum. In the last five to ten years there are all kinds of crazy things happening at school—from gangs to drugs to bullying. Some kids will turn a deaf ear to their parents. Some of my nieces and nephews feel their parents are trying to keep them from doing certain things and they interpret it as meanness. But in many cases, parents are simply trying to keep their children out of harm's way by trying to be their eyes and their ears in an effort to place protective boundaries around their children.

These are some of the things I try to emphasize to my audience and again to anyone who reads this book. Sometimes kids will listen to an athlete they admire, but athletic success is just a platform to reach young people. I try to tell kids that their parents are looking out for them and don't want them to make serious mistakes. Part of my purpose is to not only help the kids, but their parents as well. Hopefully, I can make everyone think about improving their home game. Sometimes the light doesn't come on right away, but that's okay, as long as they listen. I always pass out small notebooks with some of my advice written in them so they'll be reminded of the things I've said. I may never see some of those kids again, but I always want to make the most of the moment.

GEAR UP and Aim High

I once spoke to a group of girls in a holding facility. They were just 13, 14 or 15, and all were awaiting court dates. There was one girl who used to play basketball. She had quickness and talent, but somewhere along the line she got off track. What caused it? Abuse at home? Maybe abuse by a boyfriend? I've thought about those girls a lot since I met them. I didn't preach to them, just told them they had their entire lives ahead of them and it wasn't too late to fix what went wrong and to get back on track. You all have the potential to be great mothers, great teachers or great leaders, I told them. It's never too late to become the women you really want to be. If you learn from your mistakes, they become valuable life lessons. I just hope what I said reached some of them.

Young men and boys need even more encouragement if they come from urban minority communities. So many young people today need empowerment. Many go through a great deal at an early age and I want to help them at the crossroads in their life. When they're between about the ages of 10 and 12, it's a great time to connect. By the time they begin their teenage years, many have been exposed to so much negativity, but it's never too late. I always strive to be with kids I can help shape, before they are in too deep. That's why I'm happy to be associated with two programs that are working their way into some schools in California and are further enabling me to continue my ride of a lifetime.

GEAR UP (Gaining Early Awareness and Readiness Undergraduate Program) allows kids to win money toward college. They can get at least $2000 toward college while still in junior high school. This is a federally funded national organization and the only one to give college scholarships to kids at that early age. It is specifically for kids who start thinking early about attending college. I'm happy that they are allowing me to share my program with GEAR UP kids, telling them about the importance of a solid foundation and how best to deal with peer pressure, among other social challenges.

Ruthie with students who participated in her Aim High program

The GEAR UP program is generally for middle school or junior high students. Usually, the targeted groups are kids from lower income homes, many African-Americans, and the hope is that the program will give them a better chance to escape poverty and achieve success. Each kid needs constant attention. I began working with the kids at Valley High School in Elk Grove, California, for the past two years. When the principal, Michael McDonald, asked me to help out, I didn't hesitate.

He said my heart was in the right place. Shelly Davis, the coordinator of the Valley High and Northern California regional GEAR UP program met with me and loved my Aim High Program. She felt that my program would be great for Jackman Middle School and other middle schools. In addition, I've adopted Martin Luther King Middle School in Sacramento, California. Mr. Williams, the school principal, Colonel Harris, Coach Michael Shaw, and staff have done an amazing job with the children. Like the GEAR UP Program, Principal Williams and his staff talk about many of the same things—dealing with adversity, overcoming roadblocks, and turning NO into Yes. Hopefully, this book will serve as a reference to guide even more youth I cannot physically reach. It gives them the whole package, including my story with all the ups and downs, and how I came to be where I am today.

The Ride of a Lifetime

The secret of a successful ride is to stay on course. After all, it's your life we're talking about. There will be times when you feel as if you're going 80 miles an hour, but suddenly you have to slow down to 40, or maybe stop for a roadblock. Or you may even have to take a detour. If you stay on course, sooner or later you'll get back on that straight road and be traveling at 80 miles an hour once again, headed straight for your destination.

I've had an amazing ride. Sure, there have been ups and downs, peaks and valleys and times I thought I'd have to get off the road completely. But whenever that happened, I reminded myself of Dad's teachings, especially about perseverance, working hard and not giving up. So it has been a beautiful ride, mainly because I'm content with who I am. My struggles have helped me become a better person and have enabled me to prepare for the bumps and roadblocks I know will come. No matter what might get in the way I still know my destination.

I have always sought out and found people along the way who have helped me stay on course, not only my family, but teachers and coaches, and good friends. Young people need positive reminders about how possible it is to achieve their goals despite the odds. That's part of the ride. So is having family by your side, older siblings or a friend you can share with. They always give you food for thought. Sometimes you may share with someone standing in line at Wal-Mart. Maybe whatever you said will have made their day better. Life is often about the small things, the intangible things money can't buy.

No matter what happens, always keep your eyes on the finish line. If you continue to get up when something knocks you down you're on your way to making good things happen. But if you don't get up, you won't be able to see what's ahead and then you won't have a chance to reach that place you want to be. Getting up and continuing the ride is a mindset, an attitude. And, as I've said so many times, that's something you try to develop early and enhance as you grow and mature.

I envision the rest of my life being involved in community, mentoring and developing youth, whether through coaching and/or school programs. That's my passion, the thing that gets me excited. When I wake up each day, I know that's my purpose in life. When I help people follow their passion it will eventually drive them to the right place. There are people with good jobs who make a nice living, but their work isn't a passion with them, only something they have to do. Some find their passion early; others find it later in life. There are retired people who now follow their passion as volunteers.

🌣 *The secret of a successful ride is to stay the course.*

It's a perfect situation if your job is also your passion, but if it isn't you may still follow your passion on weekends. For example, you may be a business executive during the week, but your real passion may be to help and inspire older people. That's something you can do on weekends. You may even be a very good athlete, but your real passion is music. My friend, Wayman Tisdale was a perfect example. He was a huge collegiate basketball star at Oklahoma, and then played 15 years in the NBA. All the while, he took his guitar with him and practiced playing, composed music and entertained his teammates. This kept him in a great state of mind. Once his career ended, he became a well-known smooth jazz guitarist with a number of hit recordings. He was truly an amazing performer. Tragically, he died several years ago of an illness, but never lost his faith and his desire to make people happy until the day he died. The bottom line is that you must keep looking for your passion and purpose. The thing that will give you the best ride of a lifetime. Once you find it, you become a fuller, more complete person.

There are people who work for 35 or 40 years and suddenly ask, "What have I done with my life?" They wind up feeling empty, as if they hadn't accomplished anything. That's because they never found their true passion. If you follow your passion and your dreams, you'll undoubtedly wind up helping people around you. Passion gives you the ability to empower others.

Basketball was an important part of my life and I achieved a great deal as a player. It also gave me a platform and that helped me move into another area which I truly love. Others who play basketball continue to love it and wind up coaching or teaching basketball. It's their passion and that's fine. As long as you retain your joy and passion with anything, you'll be passing that along to others. Your passion may help people achieve in other areas. I've always been a person of passion. People have told me they were inspired by the way I played basketball because I always played very hard. Doing anything that way will inspire others. As you pursue your happiness and dreams you'll find out who you are. That's the way it happened with my friend, Beatrice, in Italy. She was a housewife who raised two kids and when she was 40, she suddenly began running and found her passion. Her inspiration, she said, came from seeing how fit I was. Soon, she was not only very fit but thinking about running marathons. Now she has an organization—a club for young women who want to run and compete. It's the only organization in Italy, with a group of ladies who train together and enter running competitions.

Ruthie Bolton, 2011

As soon as she found her passion, it began to define her, and also showed her how she could make a difference in other people's lives. Her husband, Franco likes to joke with me, telling me I helped create a running monster. But she is extremely happy with what she's doing and has passed that on to other people while keeping them, and herself physically fit. She still finds it hard to believe that she discovered this so late in life. But as I've always said, it's never too late. So keep looking and you will find your passion no matter how old are you are.

I've had so many good things happen in my life, especially coming from a tiny town with 19 brothers and sisters that I can surely say I've been on the ride of a lifetime. It started simple, just loving the outdoors as a kid and playing with my brothers and sisters. I enjoyed that simple life so much that I went to bed thinking about it and woke up the same way. I couldn't wait for the next day to begin.

Life with my family was also unforgettable. I have so many memories of my mother and dad, my siblings and relatives. There were so many little moments for all of us, working, playing and praying together. I'll never forget my dad's quick little sermons, his encouragement and wisdom, and the way we all traveled in cars to church every week.

During that time I was learning so much from my dad, getting a solid foundation even before I fully realized how much that meant. I'll never forget basketball in my high school years, when we were so dominant that we lost only six or seven games the entire time I was there. The car accident with my dad is another lasting memory. Sometimes I still can't believe I survived after being thrown from a moving car into a ditch when I was 17. It took my dad 20 minutes to find me. God must have had another purpose for me because I could have easily been killed. Now, it's an integral part of my story.

My experience with the U.S. Olympic Team was unreal. That's something I'd do over again right now if I could. We were like family, working and playing together, and seeing the fruits of our labors result in a pair of gold medals. It's all part of the journey and now I feel I'm in the second phase of it. What I'm doing now, working with kids and conveying my thoughts to them, is something that makes me extremely proud.

Last, but far from least, is having my children. That experience puts an exclamation point on everything. It helps complete the circle, along with teaching and inspiring young people. When I named my daughter Hope it stood for something—Holding On with Purpose and Enthusiasm. Just another reminder of what I stand for. And I added Linwood (Christofer Daniel Linwood Bolton) to my son's name in memory of my dad, just another way in which he'll always be with me. Now they are both a big part of my ride.

Some Final Thoughts

I firmly believe everyone can have *The Ride of a Lifetime* if they work to make it happen. My ride, for example, isn't defined by persevering to play at Auburn University, making the National Olympic Team, winning two gold medals, or even being inducted into the WNBA Hall of Fame in 2011. That's just a part of it. Of equal importance are roadblocks such as tearing my ACL and certainly losing my mom and dad. Those were the storms of life. But, I knew the sun would shine once again and, sure enough, it did. It's overcoming the challenges that shape you and take you to new heights.

No one should ever give up. You've got to keep trying and stay on the path to creating your own ride of a lifetime. The greatest risk to success is to take no risk at all. You won't discover who you are without reaching higher than you ever thought you could reach and without going down the road less traveled.

Let me close with some words my dad gave me. I believe he took them from several sources and combined them to make them his own. In fact, he taped them to my door one night and I've kept them ever since. They are well worth reading many times, especially when you feel you need some inspiration. Here they are.

LIFE

- Life is a gift, accept it.
- Life is a challenge, meet it.
- Life is an adventure, dare it.
- Life is sorrow, overcome it.
- Life is tragedy, face it.
- Life is a duty, perform it.
- Life is a game, play it.
- Life is a mystery, unfold it.
- Life is a song, sing it.
- Life is an opportunity, take it.
- Life is a promise, fulfill it.
- Life is a struggle, fight it.
- Life is a goal, achieve it.
- Life is a puzzle, solve it.
- Life is beauty, praise it.

ABOUT THE AUTHOR

Ruthie Bolton (www.ruthiebolton.com) is a two-time Olympic Gold Medalist, and the original franchise player for the WNBA Sacramento Monarchs professional basketball team. She has scored over 2000 career points. She is 4th on the WNBA's all-time 3-pointer list. Ruthie Bolton is the only player in the history of the Monarchs to have her number retired in Sacramento's Arco Arena. Ruthie has been on the cover of Sports Illustrated. She's been a guest for Regis Philbin and David Letterman, and, she's even done a Nike television commercial. She was inducted into the 2011 Women's Basketball Hall of Fame.

Here are just a few of Ruthie's career accomplishments:

- 3 SEC Championships
- 2-time Olympic gold medal winner
- WNBA superstar
- WNBA Legend
- International superstar (Italy, Turkey, Hungary, Sweden)
- Sacramento Monarchs Jersey #6 RETIRED
- Auburn Tigers Jersey #25 RETIRED
- Role Model
- First Lieutenant, US Army

Chronology

1967	Born May 25, 1967 to Linwood and Leola Bolton, the 16th of 20 siblings
1984-1985	Led her high school to two consecutive State Championships (Mississippi)
1985-1990	Attend Auburn University; obtained B. A. Degree in Health Promotion and Wellness
	Helped team win two Final Four Championships; compiled a record of 114 wins, 12 losses
1987-1997	Served in the US Army as First Lieutenant
1990	World University Games Championship
1991	USA Player of the Year
1991	Goodwill Championship
1994	World Championship Team (Bronze Winner)
1996	USA Olympic Team Gold Medal
1997	Alabama Singston Award for Unsung Heroines
1997	Drafted for the WNBA Sacramento Monarchs
1998	World Championship (Gold)
1999	WNBA All-star
2000	USA Olympic Team Gold Medal
2001	WNBA All-star; 2 Ball Champion
2005	Sacramento Observer Woman of Excellence Award
2005	Monarchs Jersey Retired
2005	Make a Difference Award
2006	WNBA Honorable Mention All Decade Team
2011	Named WNBA Top 30
2011	Women Hall of Fame Inductee
	...and a host of Community Assistance Awards